D0620486

DESMOND MORTON

N D P
The Dream of Power

Hakkert • Toronto • 1974

To Ruth and Terry Grier

Cover design by R. Mitchell Design

International Standard Book Number Cloth: 0-88866-551-2
                                    Paper: 0-88866-552-0
Library of Congress Catalogue Card Number 74-80410

Printed and bound in Canada

A. M. Hakkert Ltd., 554 Spadina Crescent, Toronto, Canada M5S 2J9

37

Contents

List of Photographs

Picture Credits: Federal NDP (pp. 16, 26, 74); Ontario NDP (cover, pp. viii, 42, 58, 136); Saskatchewan NDP (p. 112); Manitoba NDP (p. 102); Public Archives of Canada (p. 2); Information Canada (pp. 118, 158); Gaby of Montreal (p. 58); Julien Lebourdais (p. 74); A. Simon (p. 2); Terry Mosher (p. 136).

Foreword

The New Democratic Party is a curious phenomenon. Isolated in the great sea of free enterprise North America, it seems alien. Yet compared to European social democratic parties, the NDP is distinctively North American, indebted as much to populism as to European socialism. Most Canadians do not vote for the party, but many of the same Canadians boast to their American neighbours of the civilizing influence the NDP has had on Canadian politics. Members of the party belong because they believe Canadian society needs changing; their greatest frustration lies in discovering that they are treated like the Mounties and the Montreal Canadiens, important culturally but somehow not quite serious.

Walter Young's history of the CCF, predecessor to the NDP, argues that the CCF failed because it never became part of the Canadian mainstream. The NDP has been more successful, but except in certain places, such as Saskatchewan and Northern Ontario, it remains slightly eccentric, not quite acceptable. Members of the party are so conditioned by this role that they feel uncomfortable when confronted by power, the tangible evidence of having arrived. For many New Democrats the exercise of power seems in itself to be a sellout: witness the abuse which Premiers Schreyer, Blakeney, and Barrett have received from their own party.

What I am suggesting about New Democrats is a degree of introspection quite foreign to Liberals or Conservatives. Only New Democrats spend time wondering whether they are really central to Canadian culture, or whether they will be corrupted by power. This navel-gazing has prompted a cottage industry of the left, a whole series of earnest literary magazines, from *Canadian Dimension* to *This Magazine* to *Canadian Forum*, which keep themselves politically relevant by attacking the deviationism of the NDP. One can only describe the exercise as literary sado-masochism, equally pleasurable to the purveyor and the receiver. New Democrats have always taken a perverse pleasure in believing the worst about themselves. They are sometimes embarrassed to discover that the worst is not true.

Desmond Morton's account of the NDP is a refreshing change because it treats the party as a party, anxious for political power. At the same time he never falls victim to the cynicism of so many commentators, who assume that the desire for power must have killed the "movement" in the NDP. The quality of Morton's history lies in the clarity with which he expresses the social democratic determination to fight for freedom and equality through parliamentary means, with all the confusion and compromise that that implies. Samuel Johnson, in a comment of singular maturity, thought that a foolish consistency was the hobgoblin of little minds. It is a mark of great political maturity to be able to accept half-measures, inadequate compromises, and constant defeat while remaining true to goals which may not be realized for generations. Desmond Morton shows what the struggle is actually like, but he also provides an eloquent statement of what we are struggling for.

Gordon S. Vichert
Secretary, New Democratic Party of Ontario

Introduction

Conventional wisdom and academic political science have generally agreed that democratic socialism has no real future as a political option in North America. In the new world, presumably, the twin socialist ideals of liberty and equality are to be achieved without the old world doctrine of the class struggle.

Since 1961, like its predecessor the Co-operative Commonwealth Federation, the New Democratic Party has attempted to defy that dogma. Launched amidst the high enthusiasm of the largest, longest political convention in Canadian history to that time, the NDP learned, as its leaders had privately feared, that it was not destined for easy victories or early triumphs. Instead, it took time to come to terms even with the urban, working class constituency it had been specially designed to win. In the process, it had to learn much about the visions and ideals Canadians could be persuaded to share.

By the end of 1973, the New Democrats could claim the support of between a fifth and sixth of the Canadian electorate. They had become the government in three of Canada's ten provinces and had even elected the parliamentary spokesman for the vast Northwest Territories. They had survived disillusionment, disappointment, divi-

sion and numerous obituaries. Like other major institutions, the NDP was still changing; unlike some of them, it seemed unlikely to disappear.

In *Canadian Labour in Politics*, written barely five years after the New Democratic Party had come into existence, Gad Horowitz predicted that, if the party had not reached major status by 1976, its architects might well reconsider their creation. This study is a preliminary contribution to that new evaluation. It is based on the conviction that the New Party movement was launched to provide Canada with a majority party of the democratic Left; that is the standard by which it should be judged. Unashamedly, it spends more time in the backrooms of the party than on its platform utterances, and on Ontario and Quebec, rather than on the western provinces, for it was central Canada that was the NDP's special target.

Historians who tread too closely on the heels of the present are likely to be kicked in the teeth. The dead have few to defend them; the living are easily aroused. Pioneers in a field can be confident only that others will improve on them. The present study is based essentially on party minutes and records, on newspapers and other products of contemporary journalism and on limited personal involvement. It is not a work of objectivity because it lacks the two pre-requisites — ignorance and omniscience. The risks seem worth taking because New Democrats themselves should consider their collective experience before it has passed into oblivion and Canadians, as a whole, deserve a fresh insight into the complex reality of their political culture.

In 1964, when I started to work for the NDP, I met the first of some of the remarkable people who had given their lives to the labour movement and to the democratic Left — rarely distinguishing between the two. Jim Bury, Gord Brigden, "Doc" Ames, Bob Mackenzie, Anita Devillez,

◁ T. C. Douglas at an NDP candidates' meeting in Toronto, 1965. (Ontario NDP)

Martha Miike, Gwen Emby, Jurgen Hesse, Marg Bishop and Ellen Adams, together with countless other valiant souls, will not find their names in this book. They must be content with the knowledge that it would not have been worth writing without their quiet struggle to make Canada better for people they will never know. Among them, I must include my wife Jan, a second generation socialist whose energies have never been held back from the cause in which she believes.

In writing this book, I have temporarily pre-empted the work which someday will be done properly by my good friend, Terry Grier. Armed with imagination, common sense and self-mocking wit, he played a greater role in the achievements of the NDP during the Sixties than anyone this side of posterity will probably acknowledge. To him and to Professor Kenneth McNaught, Marion Bryden, Gordon Vichert, Lorne Ingle, Norman Allen and many others who provided guidance and information, I remain forever grateful. They are, of course, in no way responsible for the lapses. As usual, I have been the grateful beneficiary of my publisher, Alan Samuel, and of Joan Murray and Valerie Stevens. Perhaps, too, I should acknowledge my students at the University of Toronto, for whom this book has been written. Finally, I acknowledge my debt to my family for generously sharing the sacrifices which authorship imposes.

N D P
The Dream of Power

"In the Political Nursery," a cartoon by Racey in the Montreal *Star*. The birthpangs of the CCF included a bitter breakaway by the United Farmers of Ontario and the doctrinaire intransigence of the party's labour-socialist wing. (Public Archives of Canada) ▷

CCF leaders at a camp in the Jewish Workmen's Circle, August 2nd, 1936. In the front row, second from the left, Clarence Fines, fourth from the left, M. J. Coldwell, Sophie Lewis, J. S. Woodsworth, Lucy Woodsworth, Grace MacInnis, David Lewis, unknown and Angus MacInnis. (A. Simon) ▽

I. Background

"... I am convinced that we may develop in Canada a distinctive type of Socialism. I refuse to follow slavishly the British model or the American model or the Russian model. We in Canada will solve our problems along our own lines."

(J. S. Woodsworth in Regina, 1933)

What is the New Democratic Party? How did it get that way?

The answers depend on your point of view. To a political scientist, the NDP is a party of the democratic Left, advocating moderate socialist solutions for the problems of an advanced capitalist society. It is also a sectional party, winning the bulk of its support, in geographic terms, from four of the provinces west of the Ottawa river and, sociologically, from lower and middle-income Canadians, particularly those from a trade union background.

To its own members, the NDP is both an electoral organization and a political movement, pledged to the eventual transformation of society. If few members could describe either the nature or the process of the transformation, they could still dream that people might be

3

able to live in a better, more humane relationship with each other. NDP voters, on the other hand, when asked, tend to identify the party as speaking up for Canadian working people and the less well-off. Opponents insist that the NDP is merely the mouthpiece for the trade unions or for irresponsible critics of the free enterprise system. A few condemn the party as "reformist," a major barrier to a true socialist revolution in Canada.

Another and perhaps more valid way of looking at the New Democratic Party is to see it as the product of more than ninety years of working class and radical political experience and, therefore, as an indigenous Canadian institution. From trial and error came the realization that Canadian working people and their allies needed their own distinct political party, that it had to be controlled and financed, so far as possible, by its own members, that its principal battles, though by no means all of them, would be fought within democratic parliamentary structures, and that its ideology would be a broad, undoctrinaire socialism.

Of course, not everyone draws the same lessons from history. If the New Democratic Party has undoubtedly become the dominant institution of the political Left in Canada, there has never been a full consensus inside or outside its ranks about correct strategy or tactics. Some radicals have always had a taste for revolutions. Syndicalism, the doctrine that labour struggle can short-circuit the familiar institutions of parliament and government, was discredited by the Winnipeg General Strike of 1919 only to reappear in the Quebec strikes of 1972 — with comparable consequences. Lenin's success in using a tiny revolutionary elite to overthrow the Russian government in 1917 has spawned a whole spectrum of conspiratorial sects around the democratic world, including several in Canada.

What the NDP represents, therefore, is only a majority view of what the Left can and must accomplish in Canada. Its existence, like that of its predecessor, the CCF, transforms a party system which, otherwise, might be almost indistinguishable from that of the United States. Those who find Canada's distinctiveness in her conservative tradition might find just as valuable evidence in the strength of the country's radical political party.

The need for a separate party was by no means apparent to Canadian workers when, in the late 1860s, they began to form enduring labour organizations. Certainly legislative goals ranked high on their agenda: it must have seemed easier to bully politicians than their own hard-faced employers. It could also be more fun. For a time, the traditional Liberal and Conservative parties were able to accommodate the pressures. Sir John A. Macdonald's Trade Union Act of 1872 and the promised employment opportunities of his National Policy of 1878 helped to keep most of the workers in the Tory ranks during the 1870s: factory legislation from the provincial Liberal administrations of Honoré Mercier in Quebec and Oliver Mowat in Ontario helped pull the labour vote to the Grits during the 1880s. As early as 1873, union leaders had begun presenting their views to governments in what are still known as "cap-in-hand" sessions.

For reasons which still have force in broad sectors of the Canadian labour movement, many labour leaders were content with this version of brokerage politics. Political debate could be hopelessly divisive within unions, most members accepted one or other of the established parties as well as the prevailing free enterprise ideology, and union leaders might claim minor patronage rewards for delivering the vote. When more radical labour organizations like the Knights of Labour collapsed in the 1880s, the conservative craft unions, based on high dues and the scarcity of skilled

labour, survived. Most took their political philosophy from
Samuel Gompers, an ex-socialist who presided over the
American Federation of Labor from 1886 to 1924. "Stand
faithfully by our friends and reward them," insisted
Gompers, "oppose our enemies and defeat them." For the
AFL and its Canadian counterpart, the Trades and Labour
Congress (TLC), that meant, in effect, a minimum of
independent political action and as close an integration as
possible into the prevailing social and economic system.

In the United States, where individual congressmen
could more easily be pressured to ignore party lines, the
Gompers formula might have some validity; in the Canadian parliamentary system, it did not. Canadian union
leaders found that winning the sympathy of individual
politicans made little difference. Under the tight caucus
discipline imposed by Canada's form of responsible government, these individuals had little influence. Thus entire
parties and governments had to be converted and, in
practice, that was rarely possible. A growing number of
labour radicals had no difficulty in explaining why: in
Canadian politics, the division of labour was as complete as
in a factory. Professional elites provided the candidates,
businessmen furnished the money and working people
served only in the cheering section or, as the property
franchise was gradually lowered, provided a share of the
votes. From their political frustrations, a small minority of
working people developed a sharp class-consciousness.

There was another problem with the two-party system
which was more slowly perceived. It was *not*, as left-wing
slogans still proclaim, that the Liberals and Conservatives
were identical. In fact, they reflected very real historical
and sociological differences. By the 1890s, after a major
shift in allegiances, the Liberals had become, predominantly, the party of Quebec, the West and Catholicism,
while their rivals were closely identified with Ontario and

Protestantism. This helped to ensure that the bitterest debates in Canadian politics seemed to focus on issues of race, culture and religion. This obsession has regularly helped to obscure a broad agreement among Liberals and Conservatives that the economic system was best controlled by private businessmen, that workers would be paid as much as their employers felt able to give them and that poverty was usually the punishment for improvidence, self-indulgence or laziness. The limitations of a party system united on key economic issues are obvious.

Any party system reflects chosen priorities. Loyalties may be based on religion, ethnicity or even, as some apparently might wish, on sex. In Canada, a primary preoccupation of left-wing politics has been to shift political debate away from issues like language, sectionalism and nationalism to the divisions between rich and poor, between those with economic power and those with none. In the United States, partly because language and cultural differences have mattered less as a basis for party allegiance, partly because of the near-accident of the New Deal, it proved possible to convert a wing of the Democratic Party into a political vehicle for organized labour and the poor. In Canada, that has never happened.

Instead, as early as 1874, independent labour candidates began seeking and occasionally winning election to Parliament and provincial legislatures. In the 1880s and 1890s, thanks to a few labour intellectuals like Phillips Thompson, the author of *The Politics of Labor*, and to the influx of working class socialists from Great Britain, trade unions and labour candidates began to acquire a specific ideology. Obstacles inside and outside the infant Canadian trade union movement were enormous. Early labour M.P.s like A. T. Lépine (elected in 1888), Ralph Smith (1900), A. W. Puttee (1900) and Alphonse Verville (1906) drifted into alliances with the established parties merely to achieve a few tangible gains. Despite repeated resolutions, not until 1917 did the Trades and Labour Congress launch a vigorous attempt at electoral action (in anger at the government's imposition of wartime conscription) and it failed miserably. However, the seeds took root in a number of small labour parties in Ontario and the western provinces and postwar Canadian parliaments were never without a contingent, however small, of labour members. In 1921, they were joined by sixty-five Progressives, spokesmen for a movement of rural protest which had swept across Canada from the foothills of the Rockies to rural Ontario. The Progressives soon faded but the survivors joined with the labour members to form a third force in the House of Commons, the so-called Ginger Group, whose chief spokesman was the bearded, austere former-clergyman from Winnipeg, J. S. Woodsworth. Oddly enough, though a few political scientists still teach that a two-party system is the parliamentary norm, Canada has not known that blessed estate for more than half a century.

Reluctantly and hesitantly, trade unionists had pioneered the concept of a class party. Farmers, beginning with the Patrons of Industry in the 1890s and continuing through a succession of political and economic organizations, helped promote the same notion, though their chief mentor, Henry Wise Wood of Alberta, shrewdly described his supporters as an "economic group." Perhaps the most important contribution of the farmers' movement to the tradition of the Canadian left, in addition to a tradition of successful co-operative enterprise, was an intense emphasis on democratic control and on broadly-based financial support. In part, it was an infusion of the American populist experience, in part it reflected the intense individualism characteristic of the small farmer. But both pressures enforced a pattern of delegate democracy, regular consultation and strict accountability of leaders to followers which would characterize the Co-operative Commonwealth Federation (CCF) and, by inheritance, the NDP.

What the farmers lacked was a unifying ideology. William Lyon Mackenzie King, the Liberal prime minister after 1921, insisted that the Progressives were merely Liberals in a hurry and, as he discovered, he did not have to hustle very fast to catch them. Farmer and labour radicals failed to collaborate very effectively in the Twenties, largely because the trade unionists had developed a political programme, increasingly expressed as a theoretical and uncompromising socialism. Labour activists had long since moved past the TLC's "Platform of Principles," with its demands for free compulsory education, abolition of the Senate and exclusion of Chinese immigrants. Instead, in various accents and with varying degrees of vehemence, they preached the overthrow of the capitalist system.

Nowhere did early Canadian socialism strike deeper roots than in British Columbia, partly because of the influx of radical British workers, partly, as Martin Robin has argued, because of the resource-based economy of the province. Employees of the west coast lumber and coal barons could find a special relevance in the doctrine of the class struggle: they lived it daily. The socialism preached in the company towns of British Columbia and in major cities across Canada tended to be a dogmatic Marxism, attracting few converts but educating a generation of union leaders and organizers. Early socialism in Canada was uncompromisingly proletarian: it was also, visiting comrades complained, intellectually sterile and hopelessly out of touch with Canadian realities.

Part of the problem of Canadian socialists was that, like their comrades elsewhere, they really had no idea about how their philosophy might be implemented. Marx's assurances about the ineluctable processes of history were a poor guide to daily tactics. Did one push history or did one wait? The issue was seriously debated. Some socialists, particularly in British Columbia, contested and won elections in the early years of the century, only to fall foul of their more revolutionary associates. J. H. Hawthornthwaite and Parker Williams, as socialists, represented Vancouver Island constituencies in the British Columbia legislature but both eventually found it impossible to reconcile parliamentary responsibilities and the demands of their doctrinaire supporters. Many radicals abandoned politics altogether, turning to syndicalism and its weapon, the general strike. It was a strategy especially favoured by the Industrial Workers of the World (IWW), the romantic, venturesome labour organization which flourished in the western United States and Canada before the First World War, but syndicalist ideas were discussed in trade union circles everywhere. Though active syndicalists were not actually involved, Winnipeg trade unionists attempted a general strike in 1919. It was a failure. Tactics were muddled and uncertain. Strike leaders failed to understand that, by bringing the entire city to a standstill, they were challenging government authority as well as selected employers. Anti-strike citizens ensured that the authorities shared no such illusion. After two months, a major riot and two deaths, the strike was crushed.

Among the leaders imprisoned after the strike was a former Methodist minister and product of the social gospel movement, James Shaver Woodsworth. He did not need further evidence of the futility of syndicalist tactics. While some socialists had found their model in Lenin's 1917 revolution, Woodsworth had found his in the newly radicalized British Labour Party and its 1918 programme for parliamentary socialism. While fellow socialists now

preached the revolutionary overthrow of the hated capitalist system, Woodsworth insisted that change could be
achieved in Canada "by means of education, organization
and the securing by the workers of the machinery of
government." In 1921, he won a seat in Parliament for the
Winnipeg constituency he would represent until his death
in 1942. As one of the tiny contingent of labour members,
he watched with dismay the floundering, division and
eventual disappearance of the Progressives as a political
force. Learning their lesson, Woodsworth became a master
of House of Commons procedure, rejected a Liberal offer
of a cabinet portfolio, and used his bargaining power with a
minority government to extort Canada's first old age
pension legislation. His ally, another former clergyman,
was William Irvine, elected as a labour M.P. from Calgary.
The two became the nucleus of the Ginger Group, a loose
alliance which soon included Agnes Macphail, Canada's
first woman M.P.

By no means all the Canadian Left had followed
Woodsworth's lead. On May 23rd, 1921, the Communist
Party of Canada was formed at an almost cloak and dagger
meeting in a barn near Guelph. Seven months later, the
Communists gave themselves a public front by forming a
Workers' Party of Canada for which they pulled the
strings. Though the Communists resembled the innumerable sects and fractions which splintered the Canadian
Left, their discipline and conspiratorial tactics gave them
enormous advantages in disposing of left-wing rivals.
Impeded only by contradictory and ill-conceived orders
from Moscow, a tiny handful of militants destroyed an
enfeebled Canadian Labour Party and infiltrated a number
of unions before being expelled.

The Twenties were a desperate period for Canadian
unions and radicals. Dismal poverty and low wages
persisted but almost no-one seemed to care. Labour was on

the defensive against a form of industrial democracy
pioneered by Mackenzie King in his days as a Rockefeller
employee — the company union. The farmers' movements
were disillusioned by politics and disintegrating under the
solvent of high prices. When the economic blizzard swept
across Canada in the Thirties, capitalism tottered but its
sworn opponents were too busy trying to rescue the
victims to try to complete its overthrow. There was one
benefit. Radical farmers and workers slowly realized that
they had more in common than their destitution. Conferences of the scattered, quarrelsome western labour parties
had begun in 1929 and, at Calgary in 1932, they finally
found unity with farm groups in proposing "a co-operative
commonwealth, in which the basic principle regulating
production, distribution and exchange will be the sup-
plying of human needs instead of the making of profits."
The Co-operative Commonwealth Federation was born.

In the East, a group of academics formed the League for
Social Reconstruction (LSR) and provided the Canadian
Left with a version of socialism in tune with the Fabian
parliamentary tradition and, to some extent, with Canadian economic and social circumstances. At Regina, in
1933, the CCF's original eight-point programme was
replaced by a lengthy manifesto prepared by an LSR
committee and drafted by a Toronto academic, Frank
Underhill. It emphasized economic planning, nationalization of financial institutions, public utilities and natural
resources, security of tenure for farmers, a national labour
code, socialized health services and greatly increased
economic powers for the central government. To suit its
fervid mood, the Regina convention added a conclusion
asserting that: "No C.C.F. Government will rest content
unitl it has eradicated capitalism and put into operation
the full programme of socialized planning which will lead
to the establishment in Canada of the Co-operative
Commonwealth."

Despite its aggressive ending, veteran radicals like Ernest Winch from Vancouver complained that the statement was no more than pale pink, if only because it explicitly rejected violence and guaranteed compensation to dispossessed owners. On the other hand, rural leaders from Ontario and Alberta complained that the convention had been captured by doctrinaire socialists and that the Manifesto was "not the language best understood by Ontario farmers." At Calgary, a lone trade union leader, A. R. Mosher of the All-Canadian Confederation of Labour (ACCL), had appeared but he did not come back to Regina. Boldly, the CCF had subtitled itself "Farmer-Labour-Socialist" but none of the constituent elements seemed really happy. In 1934, continued flirtation of socialist groups with the Communists forced Woodsworth to dissolve the Ontario CCF but factionalism continued to wrack the party from coast to coast. In 1935, William Aberhart's Social Credit landslide engulfed the mildly sympathetic farmer government of Alberta and what had once seemed one of the most radical provinces of Canada rapidly became the most conspicuously conservative. Only in Saskatchewan, during the depression years, did the CCF find significant electoral support.

Paradoxically, it took a world war and returning prosperity to make the CCF grow. A younger, more pragmatic generation of leaders emerged in the wake of J. S. Woodsworth's refusal to compromise his pacifist principles in 1939. M. J. Coldwell, an English-born Regina school teacher, became the CCF's second national leader. David Lewis, a Rhodes Scholar, lawyer and dramatically effective speaker, became national secretary at a meagre $1,200 a year. T. C. Douglas, a young Baptist minister who had been elected to Parliament, returned to Saskatchewan to lead the CCF to its first provincial victory in 1944. For many Canadians, the war hammered home the CCF's depression message — that resources could be found to sustain full employment and a booming economy if only the will and the planning were available. In 1942, a CCF candidate upset the Conservative party leader in a by-election in the traditionally Tory Toronto riding of York South. Overnight, the CCF became an electoral force. In 1943, an Ontario provincial election boosted the party's share of the vote from five to thirty-one per cent and the CCF narrowly missed forming the government. A year later, it was in office in Saskatchewan and a Gallup Poll had indicated that the national CCF had more popular support than either of its rivals.

It seemed like the verge of victory for Canadian socialism. Instead, it was the top of the mushroom. Mackenzie King's Liberals, threatened with defeat and caucus defections to the CCF, hurried family allowances and a generous veterans' charter into law and promised much more. The Conservatives added "Progressive" to their name and strained, a little unconvincingly, to deserve the title. The business community financed a vitriolic anti-socialist campaign which did not hesitate to link the CCF to Hitler's Nazis. Even the Communists got into the act. Terrified lest democratic socialists make major gains, the Communists formed an odd, clandestine alliance with the Liberals, working effectively to split the left-wing vote in major industrial centres like Vancouver, Windsor, St. Catherines and Hamilton. In the 1945 federal election, the CCF advance was stopped in its tracks. In Ontario, where its popular support slipped back to twenty-two per cent, its legislative representation fell from thirty-four to eight.

Never again would the CCF recover the momentum of the war years. In Ottawa and in provincial legislatures from Nova Scotia to British Columbia, it provided contingents of able representatives, offering much of the inspiration and innovation to be found in Canadian politics in the stagnant postwar years. It was not enough. Falling membership, tired leaders, financial crises and declining electoral support were all symptoms of what a sympathetic sociologist, Leo Zakuta, described as "a protest movement becalmed."

Only in Saskatchewan had the CCF achieved power and only there did it survive as a major force. A unique socialist outpost in North America, it was, to the party's unmixed delight, a success story. In 1944, the province had been almost bankrupt, harder hit than any other by the combined onslaught of drought, rust, grasshoppers and depression prices. In twenty years in office, the CCF did not transform Saskatchewan into a Garden of Eden or even a socialist utopia, but it did fulfil virtually all its promises. It collected a team of brilliant civil servants and put them to work to restore and diversify the province's economy, setting firsts in Canada for hospital, health and automobile insurance and in welfare and labour legislation, creating publicly-owned industries, some of which failed, most of which proved to be successful. Moreover, the CCF in Saskatchewan managed to maintain the unique grass-roots organization which had carried it to power and, probably to a greater degree than any other democratic socialist party, the CCF in government remained accountable to its members and supporters.

Try as it might, the CCF could not make Saskatchewan a launching pad for a fresh attempt to spread its strength across Canada. In Alberta, the party made almost as little headway as Social Credit made in Saskatchewan. In British Columbia, the CCF seemed to be permanently installed as the official opposition regardless of who formed the government. In Ontario, after virtual annihilation in the 1952 election, all that proved possible was a painfully slow recovery. In Quebec, where the CCF had suffered under ecclesiastical ban during its ten formative years, there was

△ The CCF in power in Saskatchewan. From the left, Clarence Fines, provincial treasurer and architect of Saskatchewan's economic boom, T. C. Douglas, and C. C. Williams, the Minister of Labour. "A visionary could not have run Saskatchewan with brilliant success for almost eighteen years." (Saskatchewan Archives)

The CCF delegation at the conference of Commonwealth labour parties in 1944. From the left, Clarie Gillis, M. P. from Cape Breton, David Lewis, national secretary of the CCF, M. J. Coldwell, national leader, Percy Wright, M. P. from Saskatchewan and Frank R. Scott, national president. (Federal NDP) ▽

virtually nothing beyond the courageous personal leadership of Thérèse Casgrain. In Atlantic Canada, the only oasis of support for a wandering CCFer was the coal mining community on Cape Breton Island, already in sharp economic decline. Perhaps the political scientists were right about left-wing politicial parties in North America.

There was only one other possibility — a fresh look at Woodsworth's own political model, the British Labour Party. Nowhere in the world had democratic socialist parties made headway without a direct, organic link to their trade union movements. That had certainly been the case in Britain and western Europe, in Australia and New Zealand. The CCF had envisaged the possibility of effective links but, in the 1930s, most Canadian trade unionists were either tied to the Gompers tradition of the TLC or to the Communist-controlled Workers' Unity League. Not until 1938 did any labour organization — District 26 of the United Mineworkers of America, stormy petrel of the Cape Breton coal fields — affiliate with the CCF. Its move was a reflection of a wider movement in the United States, the launching, under Mineworkers' leadership, of the Congress of Industrial Organizations. Under the magic letters CIO, American unionism finally battered its way into huge, hitherto impregnable industrial plants. In Canada, the CIO mystique inspired young activists in both the CCF and the Communist party and, although initial progress was slow, wartime brought a flood of organizing victories and a massive growth in the ranks of organized labour across the country. In 1940, a merger of the national unions in the ACCL and the new CIO unions created the Canadian Congress of Labour (CCL), a rival for the more conservative TLC. Three years later, the new Congress broke with all precedent by endorsing the CCF as "the political arm of labour." A Political Action Committee (PAC) was authorized to give practical effect to the motion of support.

The CCL endorsement was a precedent of enormous importance but of little immediate value. Within the CCL and in all its major industrial unions, a bitter, remorseless struggle for control was soon raging between Communist leaders and their opponents — most of them militant CCFers like Charles Millard, Larry Sefton, William Mahoney and Fred Dowling. While they held control, the Communists effectively prevented support for their CCF rivals — often with arguments that Sam Gompers would have admired. Even when they had been defeated in all but a handful of unions, the scars remained. Victory had come too late to help the CCF at the peak of its strength and, when aid was forthcoming during the Fifties from big industrial unions like the Steelworkers, Packinghouse Workers and United Auto Workers, it could only replace the party's own failing financial resources.

In 1954, the negotiations for the merger of the TLC and the CCL began. An obvious stumbling block was the divergent attitude of the two congresses to political action. Deliberately, the CCF supporters held back from forcing the issue. Old leaders were retiring and even in the TLC a few active CCFers were rising to positions of influence. When the new Canadian Labour Congress formally came into existence in 1956, an agreed policy had been evolved in consultation with CCF leaders. Within two years, under leadership from men like Stanley Knowles and the Steelworkers' Eamon Park, the Congress would move to create a new alliance of the political Left in Canada. For the first time, most of organized labour in Canada would be invited to get involved.

In 1871, the Toronto Trades Assembly had come into being to help workers fight for a nine-hour day in a six-day week. Ninety years later, the descendants of those Toronto workers could create their own political party.

II. Foundation

In 1957, the CCF celebrated its twenty-fifth anniversary. A committee gathered photographs, recollections and a scattering of advertisements and published a souvenir booklet. To some, it looked like a slightly premature obituary. In that year's election, the vagaries of the system had given the CCF twenty-five seats — more than at any time since 1945 — but popular vote had slipped again to 9.7 per cent, the lowest point since 1940. Since 1945, the CCF had turned from thoughts of power to congratulating itself on its internal democracy, the value of its contribution, and the benevolence of its influence on legislation. Now there were doubts that the CCF could even survive as the nation's conscience. They were confirmed less than a year later. Reinforcing John Diefenbaker's mandate to govern, Canadian voters left the CCF only eight seats and a mere nine per cent of the vote. The party's most respected leaders, Coldwell and Stanley Knowles, were defeated.

The CCF's problem was no longer a secret. Where did a solution lie? To the party's left wing, the invariable answer was a return to a purer, less compromised socialism. To Colin Cameron or H. W. Herridge, the old enemies were still alive. The face of capitalism had not changed. The dominant leaders — Coldwell, Knowles, Lewis, F. R. Scott, the Montreal lawyer and poet — thought differently. The CCF could not appeal to Canadians in the prosperous Fifties with slogans and rhetoric redolent of the great depression. In 1956, after a number of false starts and a great deal of ill-feeling among CCF fundamentalists, the Regina Manifesto was supplanted by the Winnipeg Declaration, a statement which suggested that the CCF had come to terms with the reality of a mixed economy and that its concerns were with a wider world, not merely with Canada. However, as the 1957 and 1958 elections demonstrated, party images are not changed by mere prose. The handful of Liberal or Conservative voters who might burst from their parties in a rage were not in search of moderation. Veteran CCF voters could only wonder whether their cherished party had sacrificed its teeth. It was not simply the Regina Manifesto which tied the CCF to the Thirties; it was the name, the faces, the utterances, the ever-present righteousness — the entire image of the party.

A year before the 1958 electoral debacle after initiatives from CCF leaders, the Canadian Labour Congress executive had begun to decide its stand. At Winnipeg in April, 1958, the CLC convention endorsed, with barely a dissenting voice, a call for "a fundamental realignment of political forces in Canada in ... a broadly based people's political movement which embraces the CCF, the labour movement, farmer organizations, professional people and other liberally minded persons interested in basic social reform and reconstruction through our parliamentary system of government." Three months later, a shaken, demoralized CCF almost unanimously accepted the invitation. A joint CLC-CCF committee, soon rechristened the National Committee for the New Party (NCNP), was formed with ten members each from the party and the Congress. In due course, ten more members were appointed, representing the other elements that had been invited to participate. When the farm organizations bluntly announced that they were not interested, the NCNP promptly dreamed up the institution of the "New Party club" which farmers could organize on their own. The device was even more appropriate for the professionals and "liberally-minded." Staff and organizers were appointed and, by the summer of 1961, a newsletter optimistically claimed 8,500 members in three hundred clubs, most of them clustered in Ontario and Quebec but one as far away as London, England. Of the ten "club" members added to the NCNP, four represented agriculture and the rest were middle class professionals.

Three years is a long period of gestation, even for a national political party. It was, a later NDP pamphlet grandiloquently put it, "the longest, largest nation-wide teach-in in our history." In the unions and in the growing New Party clubs there was enthusiasm. Canadian politics were becoming interesting. Economic recession brought rapid disillusionment with the Diefenbaker government. Workers were dismayed by rising unemployment, reaching half a million jobless in the winter of 1960. The urban middle class deplored the government's perennial indecision. Union leaders saw little improvement in the Liberals, particularly after the Smallwood government in Newfoundland crushed a loggers' strike and virtually drove free trade unionism from the province without protest from the federal Liberals.

Only among CCFers was there a growing resistance. "It seems to me," complained a leading member in Nova Scotia, "that the principle we believe in and have fought for these many years is worth a little dignity and not to have to be crawling for help from people that should be with us." In British Columbia, the provincial secretary complained that New Party members were being admitted

regardless of their ideology. Alberta CCFers grudgingly
acquiesced in the arrangement only after they had founded
a "Woodsworth-Irvine Fellowship" to promote true socialism. In Saskatchewan, where the trade union alliance
promised trouble among an already dwindling force of
rural supporters, the name CCF was to survive as the title
for the "Saskatchewan Section" of the new party. Even in
Ontario and Quebec, provinces which apparently had most
to gain from a formal alliance with labour, persistent
suspicions of trade unionism grumbled at the edges of
party meetings. Douglas Fisher, one of the few CCF
newcomers to Parliament in the 1957 and 1958 elections,
predicted that the alliance would deliver few votes and
that the unions would sit on their financial resources.

The problem for Fisher and other doubting CCFers was
that they really had no alternative. The New Party
movement now had a momentum of its own — it had been
endorsed almost unanimously. In the absence of any other
constructive choice for the CCF, denunciations of corrupt
unions or allegations of abandoned principles merely
provided hostile editors with welcome ammunition.

Moreover, there was just enough success to hint that the
idea might work. In federal by-elections on October 31st,
1960, a boyish Walter Pitman, running as a New Party
candidate, captured Peterborough. If a small, conservative
Ontario manufacturing town could be captured, the
movement was on target. Early in 1961, the Quebec
Federation of Labour endorsed the New Party by a margin
of 507 to 5. To a movement perennially shut-out of
Quebec, the news sounded incredible. On June 28th, T. C.
Douglas, the diminutive Saskatchewan premier, finally
announced that he would be a candidate for the New Party
leadership. The man the organizers had always wanted was
available.

CCF conventions had been gatherings of only a few

hundred delegates, meeting annually in hotel ballrooms and halls. For the Founding Convention, trade unionists contributed their organizing expertise. From the decorations to the labour troubadour, improvising folk songs for the occasion, it looked and was professional. The new image was being fashioned. Cautiously NCNP and labour leaders attempted to ensure that it was not an image of trade union domination. The labour members of the NCNP had collected $175,000 for a New Party Founding Fund; most of it helped pay travelling expenses for non-union delegates. Careful predictions about attendance helped ensure that union delegates were outnumbered by CCF and New Party club representatives. Of the 1,801 accredited delegates, 631 came from union locals, 710 from the CCF and 318 from the clubs. The balance included M.Ps, M.L.As, members of CCF councils, labour federations and the NCNP.

For five days, in 1961, 2,084 delegates, alternates, guests and officials filled the sweltering Ottawa Coliseum. Between speeches from prominent well-wishers and procedural battles, issues which had been in flux had finally to be settled. Programme, structure, leadership and even the party's name had been debated in pamphlets, magazine articles and even a book, *Social Purpose for Canada*, published by the University of Toronto Press on the convention eve. A series of New Party seminars had been conducted across Canada as a vehicle for publicity and for genuine influence on the forthcoming meeting.

Inevitably, if the convention was far from a rubber stamp, it predominantly shared the sense of direction which the organizing committee had set. The draft programme, adopted with little amendment, was in sharp contrast with the rhetoric of the Regina Manifesto (though not with what the CCF had actually been saying for the previous fifteen years). Mindful of recent unemployment, it promised jobs, economic planning and the organized mobilization of social capital which would generate orderly growth. It proposed a Canadian Development Fund and a list of measures to regain control over foreign-owned corporations. National programmes of health insurance, portable pensions and sickness benefits, free education "at all levels to all who can benefit from it" and a steeply progressive tax system reflected the socialist commitment to equality. Elsewhere, the new party pledged itself to protect the family farm, fishermen, credit unions and even, to the dismay of veteran socialists, small business. Patriotically, it agreed to encourage Canadian culture, strengthen the CBC and give the country its own flag and anthem.

Only in two areas was there bitter debate. By the 1960s, the Canadian democratic Left was withdrawing from even its reluctant acquiescence in the Cold War and collective security. The well-advertised horrors of nuclear weapons led to demands for unilateral disarmament, first in Britain, and later, in the United States and Canada. Nuclear disarmament buttons proliferated at the convention, forming one of the few common bonds between many New Party club members and the CCF left wing. The draft programme called for Canada to abandon NORAD but to stay in NATO. It was, frankly, a compromise and it was soon subjected to a bitter, emotional attack from the floor. As they had done in so many CCF conventions, Coldwell, Douglas and Lewis came to the microphones to hammer back the unilateralists. Whatever they may privately have felt, the successors of Woodsworth would not allow the new party to go back to his isolationist pacifism.

They showed less caution in a new area. In 1960, it seemed that the ice had broken in Quebec and, by the summer of 1961, the Quiet Revolution had even reached the New Party convention. The Quebec delegation, 167 strong, was almost as large as British Columbia's. The QFL resolution had meant something. If they were to stay, there was a price, already spelled out in an article in *Social Purpose for Canada* by a prominent law professor named Pierre-Elliot Trudeau. If the new party wanted support in Quebec, it would have to be genuinely federalist and responsive to the cultural demands of French Canada. Accordingly, the draft programme had promised "equal recognition and respect" for the two national languages and cultures and a new doctrine of "co-operative federalism."

For the Quebec delegates, that was not enough. By the third day of the convention, they had persuaded the gathering to abandon the word "national" and substitute "federal" wherever it had appeared. On the fourth day, they enforced the logic of this demand by insisting that the convention agree that Canada had been created by the association of two nations. Whatever the historical nonsense of this claim, as pointed out by the CLC's research director, Dr. Eugene Forsey, the delegates overwhelmingly agreed.

Only two issues remained: the leadership and the name. Douglas's only challenger was the CCF's sole Saskatchewan M.P., Hazen Argue. His campaign reflected ill-feeling within the CCF's caucus about the New Party development and the snub Argue himself had felt when he had had to persuade the CCF's last national convention to elect him as leader. By no means a left-winger, Argue became the spokesman for those at the convention who wanted to protest, as Gad Horowitz has suggested, "against the liberalization of the party's image, against 'labour domination' and, in a sense, against the new party idea itself." The vote − 1,391 to 380 − was a predictable victory for the Saskatchewan premier and an indication of the strength of the unreconciled element in the convention.

△ T. C. Douglas, the chosen leader of the new party, is supported by
Claude Jodoin, president of the Canadian Labour Congress, and
David Lewis, former national president of the CCF. From then on,
the CLC's relationship to the NDP would be sympathetic independence. (Federal NDP)

Delegates to the founding convention of the New Democratic Party.
It seemed that the Canadian political system would never be the
same again. It would be. (Federal NDP)   ▽

The liveliest pre-convention debate had centred on the choice of a title. Some diehards had pleaded for retention of the CCF initials; others campaigned for "Social Democratic Party" and many came to like "New Party," the almost accidental name under which the three year campaign had been waged. It was short, non-committal, accurate (at least for the time being) and impossible to abbreviate into barbarous-sounding initials. Their judgement did not prevail. In the only major grassroots uprising of the convention, a handful of Ontario CCFers pushed, lobbied and manipulated their way past procedural roadblocks and won acceptance for their favourite — "New Democratic Party". It was adopted by 784 votes to 743.

By the afternoon of August 4th, weary delegates could go home, their ears ringing with appeals to work their hearts out for what they had created. Journalists filed final copy while editorial writers consulted the entrails and decided that something significant had happened. "Nobody in his right senses," warned the Montreal *Star*, "should end this week without recognizing that a new and powerful voice has been developed in the left wing of Canadian politics." Prime Minister Diefenbaker had already warned that the next election would be fought on the issue of "socialism versus free enterprise." In October, the Canadian Chambers of Commerce launched "Operation Freedom," a crude campaign, reminiscent of the Forties, directed at service clubs and school children. It would, promoters hoped, "rouse Canadians from apathy and indifference into action against the growing threats of socialism and communism."

The Founding Convention had been a success. For once, the Canadian Left had appeared in the major leagues — confident, strong, efficient, yet retaining the idealism and the basic democracy which had given it distinction. Yet, in retrospect, it had diverted attention from some basic problems; it had not resolved them. And, for many, the convention had been the end, not the beginning of their efforts. Throughout, Claude Jodoin, the president of the Canadian Labour Congress, had emphasized that the responsibility of the Congress was to bring the party to birth. Thereafter, its relations would be like those of the British Trades Union Congress and the Labour Party — sympathetic independence. It was up to individual local unions to affiliate to the party as they did to the Congress. Simultaneously, both the National Committee for the New Party and the New Party clubs dissolved. They had completed their work; the party was in existence; constitutionally they were irrelevant and even harmful to its progress.

In practice, these decisions left the party floundering for the critical first six months of its existence. The tiny CCF and New Party staffs, harried to exhaustion by convention preparations, had made no plans for the future. The money collected for the Founding Fund was gone and only a fluttering of CCF membership revenue could keep the federal organization alive. After the convention, the party leadership scattered. Douglas rushed back to Saskatchewan and the increasingly bitter battle to introduce North America's first government health insurance scheme. Michael Oliver, the new president, was in Montreal; David Lewis, the chief architect of the party, was in Toronto and Stanley Knowles was in Winnipeg, struggling to win back his seat. Only Argue and a small, slightly mutinous caucus remained in Ottawa. In Ontario, the biggest challenge for the new party, energies were reserved for a provincial founding convention at Niagara Falls on October 7th to 9th. After Ottawa, the meeting was an inevitable anti-climax.

Dissolution of the New Party clubs left hundreds of members to find their way into NDP constituency associations. Many never made the journey. Those who did too often found organizations dominated by veteran CCFers who sometimes had little patience with the newcomers. In rural areas and in Quebec, where the CCF had barely existed, the club members could presumably create their own riding associations but little in their New Party indoctrination had prepared them for that challenge. For many in the New Party movement, the attraction had been the notion of a shapeless party which they could mould to their own taste. Once the clay had set and they found themselves in a more moderate reincarnation of the CCF, they left. The bulk of those New Party people who remained active in the NDP would probably have been recruited by a revived and more relevant CCF.

In the pre-convention period, it was the trade unions that had been euphoric; the CCFers who had appeared reluctant. In the aftermath, the roles were reversed. Political involvement gave business leaders and editorial writers a fresh stick to attack the unions. Liberal, Conservative and Social Credit politicians, threatened by the new development, showed their teeth. If unions get into politics, warned Ontario's Premier Leslie Frost, they must expect to be treated politically. The Canadian Construction Association urged the federal government to consider whether the union right to check-off of dues might be cancelled since the money was to be used for a political party. In Victoria, Premier W. A. C. Bennett pushed Bill 42 into law, banning the use of union dues for any political party and abolishing check-off for any union which refused to conform. Challenged in the courts, the new law was solemnly upheld, the judges insisting that political contributions were purely an individual matter. Perhaps oddly, the courts did not extend this principle to contributions from business corporations. Meanwhile, Bennett could enjoy the consequences of his blow to the prospects of his most powerful opponents.

Bill 42 was only one of a number of examples of legislation which seemed to cut into trade union rights in the early Sixties. Having launched into politics to defend its interests, organized labour suddenly found itself more vulnerable than ever. Internally, too, there were problems. Progress toward a merger of the CLC with the Quebec-based Catholic unions was impeded not only by reviving French Canadian nationalism but also by the Liberal links of Jean Marchand and many of the leaders of the newly re-structured Confederation of National Trade Unions (CNTU). Within international unions, new strains also developed. The Steelworkers in Canada ignored opposition from their American president, David Macdonald, and affiliated; in the United Autoworkers, Walter Reuther, a former socialist, was evidently more sympathetic to the NDP than his Canadian director, George Burt, a one-time Liberal candidate. In the business-minded construction unions, there was little inclination to divert funds and energies to quixotic political ventures and some unions, notably the Teamsters and the Seafarers' International Union, had long since developed comfortable, if discreet, links with the Liberals.

Another problem affected both the labour movement and the party — inter-union conflict. To the exasperation of NDP leaders, Tim Buck, the venerable Communist Party leader, claimed that his followers would be joining the NDP and taking it over. That was unlikely. The inevitable election-time embrace from the far left still upset a few unsophisticated voters, particularly in eastern Canada but, if anything, the NDP suffered more from the attentions of youthful Trotskyites with their indefatigable conspiracies. The real Communist problem for the NDP lay in their control of a number of important unions — notably the big UAW locals in St. Catherines and Windsor, the United

Electrical Workers, with strength in Hamilton, Toronto and Peterborough, and the Mine, Mill and Smelter Workers strongholds in Sudbury, Trail and Kitimat. In each of these centres, NDP organizing was frustrated by influential Communist leaders, complicated by raids from non-Communist unions and, in some cases, utterly stopped.

Sudbury, a tough, working class city, was an example. It boasted the largest union local in North America, Local 598 of Mine-Mill — 17,000 members and over a million dollars in assets. To an outsider, the situation could only be described as bewildering. Since 1958, Local 598 had been in a state of revolt against the Mine-Mill leadership but, according to the CLC, if it wished to rejoin the main body of Canadian labour, it would have to join the Steelworkers. The local's rebel president, Don Gillis, refused. To add complications, the Steelworkers launched successful raids on Mine-Mill locals in Port Colborne, Ontario and Thompson, Manitoba, Gillis ran for the Tories in 1962 and Mine-Mill recaptured the allegiance of Local 598, all in quick succession. As long as Sudbury was preoccupied with that battle, prospects for the NDP were dim. Overall, the party's loyalty was unequivocally with its Steelworker allies; locally, solid party activists could be found on both sides of the battle. Not until 1966, when a negotiated settlement ended the struggle, could the NDP make progress.

It took time for New Democrats to understand the complex problems of its new ally. Meanwhile, the charge of labour domination supplanted the older bogeys of socialism as a favourite weapon for opponents. In the autumn of 1961, nervous NDPers summoned Claude Jodoin to calm local fears and antipathies in Western Canada. Bluff good will and a few speeches could not overcome a lifetime exposure to anti-union prejudice. With their usual excessive faith in human reason, the NDP leadership had designed a constitutional structure which refuted any logical charge of trade union tyranny and assumed that that would suffice. Indeed, it was the union leaders themselves who seemed most upset by the criticism. Whatever their own views, they recognized that most Canadians, from the judges deciding on Bill 42 to many devout socialists, shared the liberal myth that politics was a matter of purely private concern in which formally constituted economic organizations were somehow illegitimate.

Few NDP leaders could have anticipated what seemed at the time almost an act of deliberate treachery. On January 18th, 1962, Parliament began what would obviously be its pre-election session. Precisely a month later, Hazen Argue summoned the press and announced that he had quit the NDP. It was a free country and presumably he could support any party he liked. However, the Founding Convention had heard him pledge: "No matter what my role is in the years ahead, I shall speak for you, I shall work for you, I shall never let you down." Now, he insisted, his party had been captured by a clique of trade unionists. On the 21st, he repeated his charges in Parliament: "It would be most dangerous to the democratic process to have a party gain power, the effective control of which resided in a handful of labour leaders outside the House of Commons." In defecting to the Liberals, Argue had given respectability to what was becoming the most potent argument its opponents could offer against the NDP. Immediately, Argue's former colleagues picked H. W. Herridge as their parliamentary leader. An elderly and somewhat dogmatic socialist, he, at least, could be counted upon never to return to the party he had abandoned as a young man.

III. Setbacks

A political movement may survive for a time on its own dreams and self-approval. A political party must stand the test of competition. The New Democratic Party had been deliberately designed for that test but not for the non-stop electioneering of the mid-Sixties. There were four federal elections, interspersed by eight crucial provincial elections in the six years from 1962 to 1968.

In all but thirty or forty of approximately 265 federal constituencies, the CCF candidate had inevitably been a sacrificial lamb. Only the glow of spreading truth could compensate for the bruising humiliation of rejection. Underpinning the New Party movement had been the faith that, somehow, the Canadian Left could be made appealing to a host of people. At last the dreamed-of polarization would take place, leaving presumably the Liberals as a dwindling and irrelevant third party.

Illusions of early breakthrough had to ignore some discouraging evidence. The post-convention Gallup Poll indicated that only twelve per cent of the voters had rallied to the new party. Earlier that year, the Saskatchewan CCF had lost Turtleford to the Liberals and, after November 7th, when Douglas handed over his office to his Minister of Education, Woodrow Lloyd, attention shifted

33

to the fate of his former riding of Weyburn. On the night of December 13th came the shocking news: its voters had also favoured the Liberals. In Ontario, there was a further test on January 18th, 1962, when five provincial by-elections took place. Only in Beaches, a Toronto constituency that had last voted CCF in 1948, the NDP seemed to have a chance. It ran third — though only 408 votes behind the Conservative winner.

By-elections, as those who lose them know, prove nothing. For the new party, the crucial test began on April 18th when John Diefenbaker dissolved Parliament. The NDP could hardly claim to be caught unawares. It had spent three years in an unprecedented dialogue with Canadians; the complacency of the Fifties had long since dissolved. For potential working class supporters, the NDP could offer a commitment to full employment and a national medicare plan; to middle class radicals, it promised a fervent opposition to the acquisition of nuclear weapons.

However, as Murray Beck observed, "policies and platforms had little to do with the electoral decisions of 1962." For voters then and for the next four years, the dominant issue seemed to be the contrasting personalities of John Diefenbaker and his Liberal opponent, Lester Pearson. In virtuoso performances which seemed to improve with time and opposition, Diefenbaker flayed the "socialist experimenters" and ivory tower dreamers who directed the Liberal Party (and presumably the NDP). He scourged bankers and advertising agencies too, rounding darkly on "sinister interests" which allegedly threatened both him and the common people. It was marvellous theatre and it hit home, for example, with those western farmers who had once seen the CCF as their guardian against "the interests." Diefenbaker, too, offered no troubling new ideas, no dangerous alliance with the urban workers. As for the cities, they responded better to a Liberal promise of prosperity and a return to that managerial efficiency Canadians had so peevishly cast off in 1957.

The NDP might willingly match the cocky, aggressive personality of its leader against his two rivals but image contests are extravagantly expensive. The CCF had financed its central campaign largely from grudging contributions from the stronger provincial sections; the NDP federal office had access to the major national union headquarters, leaving the provinces and constituency associations to approach individual members and affiliated local unions. As a result, its net expenditure in 1962, $116,332, was almost six times as large as the sum available to the CCF in 1958. Unfortunately, even this was meagre in what became the most expensive election campaign Canada had yet experienced. After paying for the leader's tour, for a supply of pamphlets and posters, and for organizers and deposits in the weaker provinces, only $50,000 remained to buy advertising space for the party's messages.

Even the leader's tour had to be done on the cheap. While Pearson and Diefenbaker traversed the country in chartered aircraft, surrounded by staff and reporters, Douglas and a couple of aides waited at airports for commercial flights or drove with local supporters, most of whom seemed to assume that the presence of a party leader gave immunity to speed limits and even minimal standards of safe driving. Douglas was the party's greatest asset. Diefenbaker's only equal as platform speaker, he combined homey wit with a vibrant passion, capable of bringing audiences roaring to their feet. Under a folksy geniality which could disarm doubtful supporters and antagonistic reporters, there was a tough, demanding realism. A visionary could not have run Saskatchewan with brilliant success for almost eighteen years. However, there was a special worry that gnawed at Douglas as he jolted across Canada that spring. His own campaign to win Regina from the Conservatives was not going well.

Like almost everything else, that particular worry had to be left to Douglas's provincial section. Like the CCF, the NDP decentralized its campaign, leaving the critical tasks of finding candidates, organizing constituencies and distributing financial resources to each provincial NDP. Overall victory depended very largely on local efficiency, energy and experience. Obviously, Saskatchewan and British Columbia had to be equal to the task. Ontario, Manitoba, Alberta and Nova Scotia were all organizationally weaker but they could manage. Apart from Ontario, which missed four of its eighty-five seats, all of them fielded full slates of candidates. In the remaining provinces, a few organizers and the promise of deposit money helped provoke token campaigns in fifteen of the twenty-one seats in New Brunswick, Newfoundland and Prince Edward Island.

Quebec was more difficult. Despite its impressive victory at the Founding Convention, the Quebec delegaton had not returned to launch its own section of the NDP. Instead, it simply resumed its constitutional debate, discovering fresh demands and fresh discontents as its leaders struggled to remain on the leading edge of the growing nationalist and radical movement in French Canada. Despite formal support from the Quebec Federation of Labour, only a handful of local unions sought affiliation, most of them at the urging of their national offices. For all the exciting promise of August, 1961, Quebec was apparently still a desert for the new party. In a few English-speaking constituencies on the island of Montreal, NDP associations launched vigorous but lonely campaigns; elsewhere, there was little action. Douglas did his best. On May 20th, he descended on Quebec City, paid a ritual visit to Cardinal Roy and loyally endorsed co-operative federalism and the two-nation version of Canada. Meanwhile, a few devoted organizers scoured the province, searching for standard-bearers. By nomination day, they had found forty candidates for the province's seventy-five seats — compared to the CCF's twenty-nine in 1958.

Decentralized structure and leadership hiatus after the Founding Convention meant that there was little campaign strategy. Almost the only tactical decision, to be repeated in the two ensuing federal elections, was to reserve the final weeks for major rallies, beginning in Halifax and ending in Vancouver. Though the pundits insisted that television had ended the era of mass political meetings, party leaders believed that rallies were virtually the only way of penetrating the media blackout which would descend on the party during the final fortnight of the campaign. Moreover, organizing the rallies involved a special expertise which the labour movement could contribute.

Almost to the disbelief of the organizers, the strategy seemed to work. In Montreal, newspapers recorded that 1,500 cars had formed a Douglas cavalcade and thousands of supporters had cheered as he denounced nuclear weapons. On the following day, 6,000 people packed Toronto's O'Keefe Centre and hundreds milled outside as Douglas turned his wit on Tory millionaires. On June 13th, there were 9,500 people to hear him in Vancouver. As the campaign ended, New Democrats might once again believe that Canada was moving in their direction.

It was not. On June 18th, 1,036,853 Canadians marked ballots for NDP candidates but they represented only 13.5 per cent of the electorate — approximately the share the CCF had collected in 1949. The electoral system delivered nineteen seats to the party — one on Cape Breton Island, three in Toronto, three in northern Ontario, two in Winnipeg's north end and ten in British Columbia. In Saskatchewan, the party vote tumbled lower than in any election since 1935 and, as a supreme humiliation, Regina electors decisively rejected Tommy Douglas.

Save for a few decorous regrets about Douglas's defeat, the editorial writers were jubilant. The New Party experiment had failed. The NDP had lost the farmer's support without collecting the workers. A Gallup survey after the election reported that voters from trade union homes had split twenty-three percent for the NDP, twenty-five per cent for the Conservatives and an overwhelming thirty-eight per cent for the Liberals. On the other hand, party officials, scratching hard for a silver lining, found a few traces. Even if editors had not noticed, party members knew very well that farm support had been slipping for some years — long before the creation of the NDP or Argue's defection. If trade unionists had not switched massively to support their new party, it was also true that the CCF had never won as many as six federal seats in Ontario or ten in British Columbia.

If the 1962 election had settled anything, the NDP would probably have had the leisure for the potentially dangerous pastime of self-criticism. Instead, Canadians found that they had elected a minority government — only the fourth in their history. As well, a totally new phenomenon had appeared, twenty-six Créditistes from Quebec under the fiery Réal Caouette. With four conventional Social Creditors, they formed the third largest group in Parliament, reducing the NDP to a humiliating fourth position. There was a fresh excitement in politics when governments might be ejected for their sins, and the country began to adjust to a situation which would continue until June 25th, 1968.

Thanks to the election night generosity of Erhart

Regier, a successful British Columbia candidate, Douglas was given a vacancy to return to Parliament as M.P. for Burnaby-Coquitlam. By then, it was apparent that another general election would not be long postponed. The bubbling fiscal problems which had plagued the Conservatives during the 1962 campaign continued and politicians who had boasted of booming prosperity had to announce a sudden austerity in public spending and re-acquaint themselves with the mysteries of balances of payments. More serious for a government already condemned for apparent indecision was the bewildering confusion about whether or not Canada was formally committed to purchasing nuclear warheads for a new family of military weapons. Among political insiders, faith in the credibility of the government and its prime minister dwindled rapidly and the issue was highlighted after Mr. Pearson, freshly back from a trip to Washington, unilaterally reversed his party's stand and informed a Scarborough audience that a Liberal government was duty-bound to honour Canada's commitment to accept the deadly warheads. In Ottawa, exasperated Tory ministers began to hand in their resignations. The *Globe and Mail* reported a plot in the business community to dump Diefenbaker as Conservative leader. After defeat on a crucial supply motion on February 5th, the Prime Minister dissolved the House of Commons and led his divided and demoralized party out to meet the people he always claimed to understand.

The election result seemed to be a foregone conclusion. In October, 1962, the Liberals could claim forty-seven percent support in the Gallup poll and, if their strength had slipped a little since, it was still enough for a comfortable margin of victory. Almost every major Conservative newspaper in the country deserted to the Liberals and, to judge from their cacophonous outrage, it was easy to believe that the country would follow suit. Instead, the raging Diefenbaker offered an even finer one-man performance than the year before. If possible, as the sworn enemy of nuclear arms, Yankee imperialists and the eastern elite, he was even more effective in appealing to alienated CCF voters, than to traditional Conservatives. The speeches in which he had denounced opponents as soft on Communism and promised to roll back the Iron Curtain were forgotten now that the Prime Minister and his prairie lieutenant, Alvin Hamilton, were standing on guard against the Americans and their Liberal allies. However extraordinary such a posture might seem to close observers of politics, a great many ordinary voters found in Diefenbaker an effective evocation of their own frustrations and indignation. On the other hand, the Liberals appealed more effectively than ever to those who wanted to end the Diefenbaker political farce and who recalled the day when their country had apparently been prosperous at home and respected abroad.

For the NDP, caught between the smooth, self-confident Liberals and the embattled prairie populist, it was hard to find room. In 1962, the party had at least been a novelty; now it felt blanked out by the news media, apparently convinced that third parties were merely a nuisance. Almost instinctively reverting to a typical CCF response, the NDP could only offer the purity of its principles. On the nuclear issue, both the Liberals and the Conservatives had switched sides: the NDP had remained steadfastly and eloquently opposed. For many, nuclear disarmament had become a moral crusade — an affirmation of life against the cruelly anonymous forces of destruction — and, if it did no more, the issue persuaded candidates to stand in ridings where they now knew they had no chance while others opened their cheque books or agreed to knock on doors during bitter late-winter weather.

Financially, the election was a disaster for the party. Most provincial sections were still collecting membership dues and unions, which had spent prodigally by their own standards in 1962, had little left to spare. The NDP's central campaign had barely $70,000 to spend and even a meagre national advertising campaign was scrapped. There were a few compensating blessings. The earlier campaign had trained a small army of volunteers and the nine-month interval was not long enough to render the contact lists obsolete. With as much encouragement as the tiny federal office staff in Ottawa could provide, most of the provincial sections wearily got to work.

In one province, the nuclear issue seemed especially promising. In Quebec, the Conservatives were no longer an alternative. Intellectuals and labour leaders who could stomach neither the pro-nuclear Liberals nor the right-wing contortions of Réal Caouette, took a second look at the NDP. On February 25th, Gérard Picard, a diminutive labour leader who had transformed the Catholic syndicates into militant fighting organizations, became the NDP's Quebec leader. A number of Quebec intellectuals, among them Pierre-Elliot Trudeau, editor of *Cité Libre*, endorsed NDP candidates. In *Le Devoir*, Jean Pellerin insisted that the election was a battle between "la grande bourgeoisie" and the ordinary people. By the end of the campaign, the NDP boasted a total of sixty candidates in the province. It had never seemed stronger.

More than ever, Tommy Douglas was his party's chief campaign weapon. Once again, he and a couple of advisers criss-crossed the country in the economy class cabin of airliners, occasionally being marooned by winter snow or fog. Though he protested that the issue of the election was not anti-Americanism, he obviously felt comfortable as he tied together the arms issue, the Liberals and the power of American-controlled businesses in Canada. If Liberals

wanted to refute charges of dependence on American corporate contributions, he told a Saskatoon audience on March 10th, let them open their books. With an apparent opportunity for gains in Quebec, Douglas offered a "council of confederation," with equal French and English-speaking membership, as a continuing forum for bicultural issues. A month later, he assured a Montreal audience that the NDP supported a tax-sharing formula which would give the provinces fifty per cent of direct tax receipts. Neither notion, incidentally, could be found in the party's programme.

Once again, the NDP campaign wound up with a nation-wide series of rallies. In Toronto, the local organization strained to top the previous year's O'Keefe Centre meeting by hiring the gigantic Maple Leaf Gardens and packing it with a precisely counted 15,842 people. Others were turned away. Not even a unanimously hostile local press could ignore that accomplishment but it responded with a drumfire emphasis on the need for stable government which, in the view of party organizers, began chopping into the NDP vote a week before election day. In most constituencies, there was little of the exhilaration of the previous year; the NDP was now an embattled minority and the members knew it.

So did the voters. On April 8th, the party won 1,037,857 of them, almost precisely the vote of the year before, but almost everywhere the NDP lost support, from a fraction of a point in British Columbia to a dismaying four per cent in Saskatchewan. The outpost in Cape Breton fell. So did Vancouver Burrard and the former CCF stronghold of York South, where David Lewis was abandoned by his more prosperous Forest Hill constituents. Across the country, the only consolations were a new seat in Hamilton and a tiny surge of support in Quebec — less than three per cent. If the "grande

◁ Tommy Douglas at Maple Leaf Gardens, Toronto. During the first three general election campaigns, NDP strategy called for mass rallies in major cities, largely to compel the news media to pay attention to the new party. (Ontario NDP)

bourgeoisie" and the people had differed, the people had gone off with the Créditistes.

In fact no party could draw much pleasure from the 1963 election. If the Liberals had won, something in Mr. Pearson or his campaign helped the party to tumble a full six per cent in Gallup standing by election day. In Quebec the Liberals had not received a smaller share of the votes since 1882 and, across the prairies, they had elected a bare three members. If the Conservatives had been saved from disaster, it was because of the efforts of the man the party's eastern leaders now despised. Even Social Credit had lost six seats and tensions among the survivors were beginning to tear the group apart. Perhaps the NDP, like the CCF before it, would accustom itself to the small mercy of merely surviving.

Indeed, there was something of the mood of a CCF revival when the party gathered in Regina in August for its second national convention. The air was thick with memories of the famous Manifesto of thirty years earlier. It was this nostalgia, as much as the baking heat, which led Walter Young, a former New Party member of the NCNP, to warn that the city was a dangerous place for the Left in the summer time. If the Ottawa convention had been a triumph for the revisionists, it was now the turn of the fundamentalists. Though T. C. Douglas successfully intercepted an assault on NATO, other convention statements on planning, unemployment, native people and pensions hinted at a withdrawal from that "mere liberalism" which both left and right-wing opponents of the NDP had condemned in 1961. For two years, it had rankled with the fundamentalists that the word "socialist" had studiously been avoided in every official utterance of the party. Now they could take comfort from a statement of "Principles and Objectives" drafted by Charles Taylor, a McGill professor who was becoming the ranking intellectual of the party, and Colin Cameron, a robustly left-wing M.P. from Nanaimo. Little of the prose could have offended anyone to the left of the Chambers of Commerce but cautiously ensconced in the second sentence was the assurance that NDP principles were "the principles of democratic socialism applied to our time and situation."

If Canadians expected something new or different from the Regina meeting, they waited in vain. The chief excitement arose from some unfinished election business. Though only a corporal's guard of Quebeckers had travelled west to remind NDPers of their "breakthrough" in Quebec, Taylor and the party president, Michael Oliver, also of McGill, made sure that the Quebec issue did not lie dormant. On the July 1st week-end, a *"conférence d'orientation"* in Montreal, designed to plan a Quebec NDP, had split into tiny moderate and nationalist wings. If something was to be salvaged, Taylor and Oliver had to be able to bring back even more unequivocal commitments by the NDP to the "equal status of the French Canadian nation and the English Canadian nation" and a promise that the party would support Quebec's withdrawal from federal programmes without financial loss. Despite a little grumbling from western delegates, the convention overwhelmingly agreed to accept both positions and an equally firm stand in favour of bilingualism and biculturalism. There was a narrower margin of support for a further demand that the party allow its provincial organizations vastly greater programmatic and constitutional independence but again Taylor and Oliver prevailed.

Indeed, there was not much the NDP could have done about it. The nationalist group, led by the former Quebec CCF leader, Michel Chartrand, met in Quebec on November 16th-17th to proclaim a new Parti Socialiste du Québec. Denouncing even a modified federal system as intolerable for Quebec, the PSQ was prepared to concede that ten virtually sovereign states could associate in a Confederation. It also agreed to confine itself to the provincial sphere, vacating the federal field to the NDP. In fact, after the brief flurry of its creation, the PSQ soon vanished.

The NDP could be more tolerant than the CCF of extended provincial rights not only because of its desperate desire to make headway in Quebec but because it had learned in Saskatchewan that a province could be a satisfying base for socialist policies. It could also afford to be philosophical about federal election defeats because party strategists were convinced that the slower but more certain route to major party status was on the basis of provincial victories. That was the foundation for Laurier's victory in 1896 and Borden's in 1911, and the NDP could follow suit. The real short-range targets for the NDP were victories in British Columbia, Ontario and, in a slightly longer term, Manitoba.

The potential of provincial power had been vividly illustrated in the previous two years in Saskatchewan as the CCF had fought doctors, the press and their Liberal opponents to institute its medicare scheme. For the medical profession across North America, it had been the crucial test struggle against "socialized medicine" and never before had the CCF faced such a sustained onslaught. When the government rejected "compromises" which would have gutted the basic purposes of the scheme, it was denounced as tyrannical. A rising hysteria pervaded the province, deliberately fostered by the doctors and their political allies until, on July 1st, 1962, virtually all of Saskatchewan's physicians closed their offices. Replacement doctors, summoned from Britain, the United States and the rest of Canada, helped provide emergency services and a chorus of opprobrium from the rest of Canada helped bring the medical profession to a more flexible mood. Within a month, a settlement had been reached and, within a year, medicare was firmly established. The achievement undoubtedly gave pride and confidence to New Democrats across Canada but, together with by-election defeats and two disastrous federal campaigns, it debilitated the Saskatchewan party and solidified its opponents.

In Saskatchewan, the CCF had demonstrated since 1944 that it could create prosperity, begin to develop an industrial base, purify a notably corrupt political system and keep its promises – copybook virtues which so far not a single other province had chosen to adopt. In November of 1962, Manitoba's Premier Duff Roblin dissolved his legislature and presented the NDP with its first provincial election opportunity. When the polls closed on December 19th, not only was Roblin securely back in office but the NDP had lost two of the CCF's ten seats and watched its share of the vote plummet from twenty-two to fifteen per cent of the total. Most painful of all, both Liberals and Conservatives had made headway in the traditional social-ist and labour stronghold of North Winnipeg.

In the autumn of 1963, it was the turn of Ontario and British Columbia. Ontario's pre-election session saw its new premier, John Robarts, introduce an armload of legislation which just managed to undercut some of the NDP's chief election planks without actually completing them – partial medicare, partial portable pensions, partial redistribution. It was a further example of that busy but unadventurous reformism which Ontario premiers since Oliver Mowat have perfected. When Robarts called his election on August 16th, most Ontarians were enjoying the summer too much to notice and it remained as dull a campaign as the premier could manage. Liberal attempts to raise scandals fell on cotton wool. New Democrats, like most people in the province, were far more oriented to Ottawa than Toronto in their political interests and their leader, Donald MacDonald, had had to struggle desperately to switch their attention to the provincial contest. Almost penniless after the two previous federal elections, the party had to send its leader to rove the province in his own car, offering lifts to any reporter who cared to come along. An organization which had been badly stretched to cover eighty-five federal ridings had to be spread over 108 provincial constituencies and it buckled under the strain.

When the polls closed on September 25th, not even the party faithful could expect a triumph. In the final weeks of the campaign, even normally Liberal newspapers had repaid the favour of the previous April by beating their drums for the Conservatives and, while this embarrassed the official opposition more than the NDP, it presaged a Tory sweep. In the circumstances, with John Robarts's candidates collecting forty-eight per cent of the vote, perhaps the party was lucky to survive. The NDP dropped a percentage point in popular support and collected seven seats in an enlarged house. A weak incumbent lost what should have been a union stronghold in Oshawa but there was some compensation in an unexpected victory at Fort William, a blessing MacDonald greeted with all his renowned ability to discover triumph in adversity.

As Ontario voters went to the polls, British Columbians were in the final stages of their own campaign. Premier Bennett had called the election without even warning some of his colleagues. His haste was probably less motivated by NDP strength than by the advent of E. Davie Fulton, a former federal cabinet minister, as the province's Conservative leader. When Fulton failed even to collect a full slate of candidates, it was soon clear that the election would be fought as the traditional right-left confrontation. However, not only was the British Columbia party relatively well-financed and organized, it was newly committed to a New Party style of moderation. As the NDP unveiled detailed plans for a premium-free Medicare plan as well as its other planks, the emphasis was clearly on constructive debate rather than walloping the enemies of the common people. Even the conservative Vancouver *Province* felt constrained to congratulate the provincial NDP leader, Robert Strachan for "his frankness, dignity and statesmanlike approach to provincial problems." By election night, NDP candidates were so elated that they were discussing cabinet portfolios. The Conservatives had flopped, the Liberals were "me too" with all parties and the Social Credit campaign — "the construction gang versus the wrecking gang" was merely the same old stuff that had given Bennett victory in previous elections.

And on September 30th, it worked again. As Social Credit piled up a fresh majority, the NDP found that it had won two new seats but lost four incumbent MLAs. More painful, its popular vote had slipped a full five percentage points and, worst of all, the losses had been in the party's lower mainland working class fortresses.

The provincial setbacks were even more discouraging to the NDP than limited progress in two federal elections. In Saskatchewan, the Canadian democratic Left had shown that it could govern imaginatively and well. Some of the NDP's most popular programmes, including Medicare and government-run auto insurance, were provincial rather than federal and, for trade unionists, it was provincial even more than federal labour legislation which needed overhaul. Yet the NDP had so far failed even to match the CCF as a vote-getter. In all three provinces, trade union areas had actually defected from 'their' party. Perhaps it was time to abandon the entire New Party experiment.

At the British Columbia convention, barely six weeks after the electoral debacle, a Trotskyite-inspired "Socialist

Caucus" briefly took over the convention and persuaded delegates to endorse a sweeping programme of nationalization and government control. When discussion turned to the recent election, party leaders were roundly condemned for their attempt to remould the party and Strachan was even denounced for the dark suit he had worn for his campaign portrait. Nonetheless, he and the moderates on the executive were easily re-elected. In Ontario, revisionism moved in the other direction. There were complaints that the 1963 federal convention had turned its back on the "liberally-minded." Val Scott, a twice defeated federal candidate who had earlier appealed for greater commitment from party leaders, delivered a letter to the Toronto newspapers calling for an "Operation Candour" to discover what had gone wrong. Farmers, he insisted, were irredeemably conservative, French Canada was hopeless and the unions had brought neither votes nor money. On December 21st, a respected Toronto journalist, Mark Gayn, revealed, in exposé fashion, that prominent NDPers and Liberals had met secretly to search out common ground. The report, which grossly exaggerated the importance and influence of the handful of individuals involved from the NDP side, nonetheless sent shivers of rage running through the party faithful and provoked resounding denials from both T. C. Douglas and the Ontario leader, Donald MacDonald.

Collaboration was harder to deny in the development of EPIC — "Exchange for Political Ideas in Canada" — a creation of the Woodsworth Foundation, an Ontario-based educational trust with links to the NDP. The latest brainchild of R. D. Sparham, the former director of New Party clubs, the organization featured intellectual collaboration between liberals and socialists, among them Douglas Fisher, the widely known maverick NDP member from Port Arthur and Pauline Jewett, a political scientist and then a Liberal M.P. Financial backing from the Woods-worth Foundation suddenly vanished, for the highly embarrassing reason that its president had embezzled its funds, but EPIC staggered on to a founding convention in Toronto on May 23-24th, 1964. With no regret from NDP leaders, it then sank without trace.

The NDP might stagger, stumble and even split in the rest of Canada — the Left had done so in the CCF era — but always there was Saskatchewan — powerful, efficient, perhaps a little smug but invariably generous and peren-nially willing to help beyond its own borders. In June of 1964, it was time for another of those quadrennial elections in which Tommy Douglas had proved his mastery over all comers. In 1963, the province had experienced a boom and 1964 promised to be even better. Medicare was working so well that, save for a few embittered doctors, it was barely an issue. Certain as any politicians ever can be of success, Woodrow Lloyd and his colleagues decided to call the election a few months early. Moreover, to avoid worrying voters who might well be satiated with political turmoil, there were no fresh programmes of reform.

If the CCF planned a relaxed, quiet campaign, so too did Ross Thatcher, the former CCF M.P. who led the Liberals. For once, he and his colleagues abandoned their slam-banging anti-socialist style, retired their amateur spellbinders, hired professional entertainers and solemnly took their advice from a shrewd Eastern advertising agency. During the month-long campaign, Saskatchewan discovered a new Thatcher, moderate, calm and occasion-ally swinging to the left of the government with promises of reduced Medicare premiums and free school books. The CCF was at first bewildered, and then amused, particularly when Thatcher's overtures for an anti-CCF coalition were rejected by the Conservatives. It was only a couple of weeks before election day that the CCF's slightly parched grassroots began to give frantic warnings. CCF canvassers were being shouldered aside on the doorsteps by a new, efficient Liberal machine. The young, unmindful of tedious depression recollections, were swinging behind the Liberals. In a few areas, government concessions to the separate schools had enraged Protestants without converting the normally Liberal Catholics. Still, it seemed impossible that the CCF could lose more than a few rural seats. Who would spit on prosperity?

On April 22nd, Saskatchewan voters did just that. Though the CCF lost less than a percentage point in its popular vote (the big fall had been in 1960), it could win only twenty-five of the fifty-nine seats in the Legislature. Except for a lone Conservative, the Liberals had the rest. After a couple of weeks' delay to see if recounts in a large number of narrowly lost seats might save him, Woodrow Lloyd resigned. The NDP was at its nadir.

IV. Elections

Riverdale was a small, downtown Toronto constituency, split between the working class East End and the slums of Cabbagetown. Twice in the Forties, it had elected a CCFer to the provincial legislature but it had become safely Conservative, the kind of seat cabinet ministers love. Federally, it had been home for George Hees; provincially, it elected Robert Macaulay, easily the ablest Ontario Tory. When Macaulay, disgusted with the triumph of lesser men, resigned in 1963, the succession was hardly in doubt. At worst, it would go to Charles Templeton, a handsome charismatic figure who had gone through a succession of careers, including a dramatically successful run at evangelism, and who now aspired to be Ontario Liberal leader.

The NDP had little hope of winning Riverdale but it did want to stop Templeton. His personality seemed to be precisely the tonic the lack-lustre Liberals might use to push their way into power, and the NDP could be badly trampled in the process. Ken Bryden, the NDP's member in neighbouring Woodbine riding, a former CCF provincial secretary and the shrewdest political mind in the party, had learned that you could find hidden votes by systematic repeated door-to-door canvassing. His colleague in the legislature, Stephen Lewis, and a party organizer, Marj

Pinney, had perfected "the system," as it was soon christened, and in Riverdale it was to be put to its most crucial test. While Templeton spent a small fortune on billboards and on radio and television time, the NDP summoned volunteers from as far away as Hamilton and Oshawa and sent them to knock on doors. When Templeton and his Tory rival spent more money, the NDP ordered additional canvasses. On September 10th, "the system" paid off. James Renwick, a radical corporation lawyer who had worked even harder than his canvassers, was the new member. A couple of weeks later, "the system" was tried again, this time in a federal by-election in the Tory constituency of Waterloo South, a mixed rural-industrial area sixty miles west of Toronto. Once again, canvassers were concentrated. Busloads of Riverdale veterans descended on the riding each week-end until, on November 9th, the NDP again pulled off a victory — this time for Max Saltsman, a Galt alderman and businessmen.

A little over a month later, in another by-election, Saskatchewan's former attorney general, Robert Walker, won back his Hanley constituency from the provincial Liberals. The province's honeymoon with Ross Thatcher had ended with remarkable speed. Apparently, all was not lost for socialism in what had once been its heartland.

There are times when one can learn a lot more from victory than defeat. During four years, the NDP could have compiled an interminable list of things it seemed to be doing wrong. It desperately needed to find that something worked. Whether or not "the system" had contributed to the by-election victories, it had not hurt. It had also given a lot of key party members a share in an experience they had rarely had before — success. Canvassing was less pleasant than discussing policy, less exhilarating than joining a demonstration. It could be disagreeably hard work but it was also politically valid and within the resources of the one element the NDP could not deny it had — people. It was probably healthy for the NDP to discover that its problems did not lie only in its programme, image or leadership but in its willingness to work.

If work was needed, the Ontario party was ready. For years, the CCF and NDP membership in the province had never pushed past 11,000. The party's 1964 convention set a target of 35,000 and endorsed a plan designed by Edward Phillips, a party vice president and a brilliant engineer, to help reach it. A year later, the party was a long way from its goal but it had met a more realistic objective of 18,000. Sustaining contributions from members, which normally totalled $40,000 or less, had more than doubled. With the extra money and with its mind set on organization, the party could launch some of the educational work it had hitherto only promised. A sprinkling of new pamphlets appeared, advising members how to cope with the rules of order or how to make silk-screen signs as well as the more predictable effusions on Medicare, the party's auto insurance scheme and the plight of Canada's native people. The party also began to expand its staff of organizers and to train its members in the techniques of Riverdale-style campaigning.

The NDP revival was not limited to Ontario. In Saskatchewan, the bitterness of the defeated CCF soon turned to fury. Thatcher's advertising advisers were barely back on the plane to Toronto before the new premier had reverted to type, swearing to carve twenty million dollars from provincial government spending and laying his axe to some of the most humane and forward-looking of the CCF achievements. Not only socialists were outraged; the Hanley by-election indicated that a good many voters shared their feelings. Farther west, the British Columbia party expelled its Trotskyites, paid off its debts and moved just far enough left to pacify its militants without alarming the middle class support which, it belatedly discovered, it had won in the 1963 fiasco. The party also seemed stronger at the centre. Its federal secretary, Terry Grier, was a cool young economist who had taken over his job just in time to bear the brunt of the two federal elections. Given even a brief breathing space, a more seasoned executive and some relief from the party's chronic poverty, Grier could begin to plan for a federal election which seemed inevitable in the spring or autumn of 1965.

Of course, the NDP revival was by no means only its own doing. Even the Riverdale victory owed something to voter reaction against the Robarts government's lop-sided majority. In Ottawa, the Pearson government's performance dismayed its own followers. Instead of the crisp, managerial efficiency which Canadians had always associated with the Liberals, the Pearson administration seemed to reel from crisis to crisis. The "Sixty Days of Decision" collapsed in a series of humiliating retreats. Throughout the spring and summer of 1964, Parliament wallowed in a debate on a new national flag which the government seemed unable to resolve. In the fall came rumblings and then eruptions of scandal, aggravated by the Prime Minister's apparent mishandling of affairs. Meanwhile, the Liberal tradition of strong central government dissolved as provincial premiers launched an extremely successful campaign to redistribute federal revenues and powers, presumably in the name of the slogan the Liberals had appropriated from the NDP — "co-operative federalism."

Quebec led the way, its demands enforced by the friendship owed to a fellow Liberal government and, even more, by the overdue realization that the province's discomfort in Confederation was real. Soon after the Liberal victory in 1963, bombs in Westmount mailboxes had claimed their first victims. When the government appointed a Royal Commission on Biculturalism and

Bilingualism, Quebec nationalists had promptly insisted that only a special associate status could possibly keep their province in Canada. The logic of the two-nation theory, first expounded to many English-speaking Canadians at the NDP's Founding Convention of 1961, was pushing closer to its only conclusion.

While other Canadians might react to Quebec demands with a mixture of uneasiness, sympathy and occasional resentment, New Democrats were more intimately involved. Electoral progress in Quebec was still a primary goal of the party, forcing it to listen to very unfamiliar sounds. To most New Democrats, French Canada's cultural demands had to be settled as fairly and fully as possible so that the entire country could cope with the shared economic problems which, to the NDP, seemed frankly far more salient. It was very difficult for New Democrats to realize that cultural issues could be involved in even such arid realms as economic planning or regional development, that Quebec's socialism had little in common with the NDP's populist Fabian tradition, that personal ambitions and careerism could be motives for professedly selfless radicals in either English or French Canada.

Plagued by ill health and unequal to the task of establishing the party in Quebec, Gérard Picard had never been more than a caretaker leader After a worried search, the NDP found his successor in early 1965. A lawyer from Quebec's rural Beauce region, Robert Cliche concealed a brilliant mind, cultural sophistication and a profound sense of his own heritage behind a bear-like exterior. A brilliant platform orator in French and English , he could not hide a warm humanity and a political acumen which had always been a rare combination in the Quebec Left. His was one of the finest and most frustrated talents made available to Canadian public life in the Sixties. In Cliche, the NDP had what the CCF had never possessed, a leader able to speak

Two major weapons deployed by the NDP in the 1965 campaign were Robert Cliche (left), the party's new Quebec leader, and an unusually large and well-directed army of canvassers who carried the party's message to the doorstep. The reward was a substantial increase in national support. (Gaby, Montreal, and Ontario NDP)

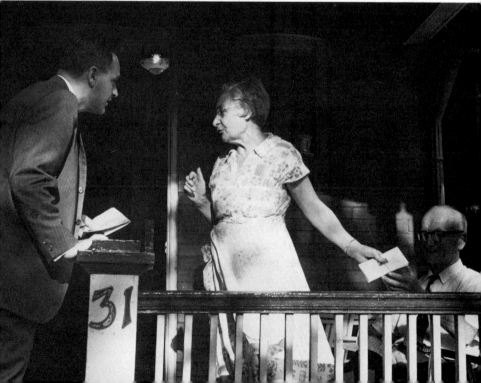

to rural and working class Quebec and to English-speaking audiences as well.

However, Cliche's presence meant that the party had to turn back to the complicated and perhaps insoluble problem of how its policies for an activist government in Ottawa could be reconciled with Quebec's insistence on political, social and economic as well as cultural autonomy. The problem was complicated by the party's constituency in Quebec. It is at least arguable that the workers who should have formed social democracy's electoral base had only a limited interest in constitutions. Certainly Réal Caouette rarely dwelt on such issues save to proclaim himself an unqualified federalist. Unfortunately, the people who tended to talk to the NDP in Quebec were not workers but, for the most part, intensely nationalist intellectuals and professionals, people for whom socialism might be an enchanting theory but to whom Quebec's constitutional grievances had become an incessant preoccupation. Through Cliche, the NDP might be able to reach a more natural milieu. First, he nonetheless needed a consistent constitutional position which would afford him credibility with Quebec political observers, to say nothing of the rest of the NDP.

The first attempt was not wholly successful. Finding a solution to constitutional problems tended to be the task the NDP assigned to Charles Taylor, and his bilingual philosophical brilliance was sternly tested. A federal council meeting on February 11th, 1965, agreed, on the one hand, that French Canada needed a strong provincial government and special consideration within Confederation but, on the other hand, that for the sake of the total Confederation, "certain basic matters had to be left to the jurisdiction of the federal government." The list, which included a dominant role in economic and social policies, was indispensable if the NDP was to promise full employment and nation-wide medicare in future elections, but there was some excuse for Paul Sauriol's complaint that, far from being decentralist, it was a major thrust toward a unitary state. And, as he reminded readers of *Le Devoir*, that was not how to win votes in Quebec.

The council statement, jointly presented by Cliche and Douglas, had been hurried before the public because, almost four years late, a Quebec NDP was actually to be formed on March 19th to 21st at Montreal. Reflecting criticism in *Le Devoir* and other nationalist organs about the NDP's constitutional stand, the 200 delegates insisted that the new group would set its own standard of autonomy, forming only an "associate" relationship and adopting its own platform plank of economic decentralization. Once again, the federal NDP faced an ultimatum from its fledgling Quebec wing that it adjust its own policy or live with the fact that Canadians would be hearing two messages from the party in the forthcoming campaign.

By July 12th-15th, when the NDP's third federal convention met in Toronto, a compromise had been worked out. Douglas and other leaders proclaimed that the party was now firmly allied with "new social forces" in Quebec. Western delegates bravely controlled their political qualms as the NDP pledged itself to work for the same rights for French-speaking minorities as the English-speaking minority enjoyed in Quebec. A complicated structure of joint federal-provincial consultation on economic planning was accepted, though Ottawa's power to initiate social programmes was justified on the grounds that some provinces might have reactionary governments. Plainly the delegates were eager to learn, to adjust their thinking and to sympathise and Cliche, who had charmed the convention, professed himself satisfied. The completeness of the educational process was, as usual, exaggerated. When delegates turned to more familiar issues — automation, consumer protection, foreign ownership, the conservation of resources — provincial rights were ignored in resolutions which essentially demanded all power for Ottawa. Perhaps the Quebec delegation was not listening or, perhaps, like other New Democrats, it was instinctively *centralisateur*.

The NDP's third convention was the prelude to its third election. On September 7th, when Mr. Pearson announced the dissolution of Parliament, even he seemed, in his television appearance, to be trying to persuade himself that it was necessary. To his advisers, Walter Gordon and Keith Davey, the reasons were quite straightforward: the country was prosperous, memories of scandal had faded, the polls were favourable. It was time for the Liberals to demand a majority. Besides, their Conservative opponents, bitterly at odds over the leadership of John Diefenbaker, were in worse disarray than ever and the NDP was no longer a threat.

Though Douglas, on the basis of the most recent Gallup poll, insisted that his party could just manage to form a government with the support of the undecideds, the Liberals had a point. In fact, the NDP had deliberately determined, with Grier's guidance, to concentrate its resources on sixty-odd priority ridings, stretching from Cape Breton to Nanaimo. In a compromise between the principle of concentration and a socialist concern for weaker brethren, organizational help, a limited national advertising campaign and the federal leader's tours would be designed to give the selected ridings as much help as possible. In another revelation which left party old-timers gasping, Douglas announced that the NDP would be spending an estimated million dollars in the campaign — a figure which was probably very close to the truth. To the party faithful and to hostile editorial writers alike, it seemed as though the party of Woodsworth and Coldwell had abandoned its virtue in a corrupt rush of affluence.

In fact, spread across Canada, distributed to printers and signpainters, landlords of committee rooms and merchants of advertising space, it was a meagre enough sum by Liberal and Conservative standards. In Ottawa, Grier had a budget of $200,000, substantially more than in 1962 or 1963, half of it earmarked for the leader's tour and to help the campaign in Quebec and the Maritimes. With a little extra help from the party's treasurer, Eamon Park, Grier found the money to run a modest four-city survey, an innovation which appalled veteran CCFers but which gave the campaign organizers greater confidence in their plans. Even more shocking to older socialists was the discovery that Grier has also retained an advertising agency to help with the campaign. The initiative had come from a bright, progressive little Montreal agency headed by Manny Dunsky. Why should the NDP be boycotted by the advertising profession, Dunsky argued, and at considerable risk to his own prospects, he took up his own challenge. The party was not an easy client. Amid suspicions from the NDP hierarchy, he and Grier helped put together a low-budget campaign designed to present a few carefully chosen messages with a mixture of bluntness and wit. To their own surprise, party regulars were delighted with the result and at least one slogan, "Let's give the two old parties a well-deserved rest — this country needs it," was regularly repeated on local party leaflets. A television commercial, attacking misleading advertising, was banned by the CTV network, owned by John Bassett, a prominent Conservative. For Douglas and other party speakers, no better illustration of corporate power could have been devised at short notice. In what, for all parties, proved a dull and issueless campaign, the NDP's advertising gave its own members an occasional badly-needed fillip.

In addition to a bolstered advertising campaign, the

federal party deployed its resources to hire full-time
organizers, pay deposits for candidates in barren constituencies and to finance the federal leader's tour. One party
representative toured the Atlantic provinces, ensuring that,
in all but Newfoundland, a full slate was fielded. Another
was assigned to the prairies. As usual, the party's research
director compiled a set of "Speakers' Notes," a guide to
current issues and the party response to them, together
with sufficient statistics to bore any but an audience of
economists.

Almost the only campaign item not prepared when
Parliament dissolved was the party's official platform.
Delayed by the convention, committees and the lassitude
of August, it was apparent that an official version could
not be prepared in time. Instead, virtually on his own
initiative, the federal secretary produced a summary of
party policies entitled, with the appropriate self-
confidence of such documents, *The Way Ahead for
Canada*. Avoiding some of the abrasive rhetoric and the
formidable length of the party's official statements, it
attempted to present NDP policy in a somewhat more
readable form, with sections on the familiar topics of
economic planning, foreign ownership, consumers' rights
and the rest. However, its main attempt was to focus on
the NDP's chief campaign issue − a sense of national
purpose. An introduction from T. C. Douglas pleaded for
new leadership to set the country moving while the final
page featured a prose poem by the leader entitled "I
Believe in Canada." The centre spread featured the party's
approach to federalism and bilingualism, embellished with
a photograph of Douglas and Cliche. Tucked into the
statement was a cautious admission that Quebec was not a
province like the others: in areas like education, town
planning and rural development, it acknowledged,
"Quebec must have the assurance that she can differ from

the rest of Canada."

There was a reason. Except, perhaps, for York South, where David Lewis was collecting most of the spare resources of the Ontario party for his attempted come-back, the NDP's biggest hopes were for Cliche, running in his native Beauce and for C. G. Gifford and Charles Taylor, running in the Montreal seats of Notre Dame de Grace and Mount Royal. Apart from the two Montreal campaigns, money for the party's electoral activity in Quebec came from the federal office and from other provinces or, to an embarrassing degree, from Cliche's own pocket. Any enthusiasm for socialist politics did not extend to paying for it. Marc Boulard, the party's Quebec secretary, later reported: "If you had ever been with me on a door-to-door appeal for money for the NDP, and seen the expressions of disbelief or amazement on the average householder's face when I explained that I represented a party which financed itself from small individual donations you would know what I mean."

Fund-raising methods were only one of many ways in which the party was culturally alien to French Canada, and its apparent irrelevance as a vehicle for reform was pointedly demonstrated by the harshest blow the NDP suffered during the campaign. After persistent rumours, three prominent Quebeckers who might have been ex-pected to be disenchanted by the corrupt, bungling Liberals, Jean Marchand, head of the Confederation of National Trade Unions, Gerard Pelletier of *La Presse*, and Pierre-Elliott Trudeau, all announced that they would be seeking Liberal nominations. After a search to find them safe constituencies, Trudeau found himself facing Taylor in Mount Royal. By helping to deny the NDP even a chance of electing a Quebec spokesman, the advent of the "Three Wise Men," as they were promptly nicknamed, was a serious setback. How serious would become even more apparent in 1968.

For the time being, however, it did not limit the NDP campaign. After a depressing start in the interior of British Columbia — making nationwide headlines only when he was bitten by a dog — Douglas soon caught his stride. If national purpose was the overall theme, there were many others — prominent among them, the virtues of minority government. To give the Liberals a majority would be to administer a tranquillizer he insisted. At evening rallies across the country, Douglas laid out aspects of the NDP programme, from an independent foreign policy to a natural resources inventory to free education so that brains, not money, would determine a student's progress. As before, the main theme was planning rather than control, and a concern — ill-requited in votes — for the poor and the elderly, abandoned in the era of affluence. In the final weeks, the pattern of huge rallies in major cities was repeated. In Montreal — where *Le Devoir* had conceded that it preferred the NDP programme to the others — Douglas insisted: "we are not one single nation, we are two. We have not one single language, we have two." In Toronto on the next night, November 5th, the party almost filled Maple Leaf Gardens to hear a warning that the Liberals were making secret plans for immediate harsh anti-inflationary measures if they won the election. In Vancouver on the following night, winding up his campaign in the crowded P.N.E. Coliseum, an exhausted Douglas repeated the charges. Then he went home to Burnaby to wait for the results.

More than ever, the experts were sure they knew what they would be. For all the gallant rearguard action of their leader, the Tories would be decimated. Pearson would have his majority and the NDP just might make small gains. After all, the pre-election Gallup poll showed the New Democrats hovering at eighteen per cent. It also suggested that the Liberals had tumbled from forty-seven to forty-four per cent in the course of the campaign, but that would be enough to hold the Conservatives, wavering between twenty-eight and thirty-two per cent.

The experts were utterly wrong. To the dismay of its operators, the Gallup reached to the limits of its built-in error. Pearson's candidates collected only forty per cent of the votes, lost all but one of their seats on the prairies, and emerged with a net gain of two. If the Liberals were victims of a lower-than-average turn-out, the NDP gained, collecting a new high — 1,381,047 votes or eighteen per cent of the total. The party lost Port Arthur (where Douglas Fisher had not stood again), but gained two seats in Toronto (including York South), another in northern Ontario's Nickel Belt and a fourth outside Winnipeg (captured by a youthful provincial member, Ed Schreyer). Bitterly, the party learned that, despite an unprecedented twelve per cent support in Quebec, it had not elected a single candidate.

Before the election, a popular Toronto columnist, Ron Haggart, had suggested that the ideal government for Canada would be a minority Liberal regime, obliged to justify its acts to a majority of opponents. Post-election pundits, full of anthropomorphic imagery, were prepared to suggest that an all-wise electorate had produced just that. It was, of course, nonsense. A voter is provided with precisely one ballot with which to express his preference for party, leader and candidate. If a voter sympathised with the Liberals, admired Diefenbaker and considered his local NDP candidate as the only fit representative, he made his choice or stayed home — a course a quarter of the eligible voters took in 1965. Obviously, disillusionment rather than conversion played a major part in the improved NDP totals but there was evidence — for example in York South — that a thorough, effective campaign could bring out votes.

Even more important for the party, in those areas where social democrats would normally expect to appeal — in heavily unionized and industrial constituencies — the NDP had finally become a force. In Saskatchewan, where the party had fallen to a miserable 18.6 per cent in 1963, it had started to climb again and, even if it failed to win a seat, it had pushed the federal Liberals back to third place.

Within a few months, the Twenty-Seventh Parliament had begun to look very much like its predecessor, with Gerda Munsinger playing the shadowy role of a Lucien Rivard and the NDP itself contributing the case of the unfortunate George Victor Spencer. It was time for the party activists to turn back to provincial politics. Unlike the Liberals and the Conservatives, the NDP organization served both levels of politics, with a basically provincial structure adapting itself to federal contests. That meant, of course, that the same members dug into the same pockets to pay for every election that came along — and in some areas, that had begun to include municipal campaigns. On the other hand, it gave local associations a continuous reason for existence and activity and it began to require a measure of inter-provincial co-operation. By 1966, a formula had been developed for the sharing of organizers and the expenses of volunteers to work in provincial elections. The originating province paid salaries of its loaned staff, the federal office paid for transportation and the host province paid expenses and made assignments. A form of cooperation which had been developing since the Saskatchewan Medicare crisis of 1962 and the ensuing campaign to develop community clinics was by now institutionalized. Ontario, with the largest permanent staff, was the chief contributor but other provinces did their best.

By 1966, a second cycle of provincial elections began. The results, like those of the 1965 election, were unsensational but encouraging.

The first province was again Manitoba. For months, Duff Roblin had been flexing his political muscles but denying that he would be a candidate to succeed John Diefenbaker when the Chief's clutch on the leadership was finally loosened. However, a fresh mandate from Manitobans would be a convenience. On May 18th, the contest began. After so many victories, no-one now believed that Roblin could be defeated — certainly not by the NDP or its ailing leader Russell Paulley. Perhaps that impression helped. When the votes were counted on June 23rd, Roblin's support had dropped from forty-five to forty per cent of the electorate, the Liberals had fallen to thirty-three per cent and the NDP was back at its pre-1962 level of twenty-three per cent. Moreover, the party had added four seats to its caucus and dropped several years from its average age. A party which had suffered from advanced years, feeble membership, chronic deficits and a fixation on 1919, began to look surprisingly young. Later that year, when Roblin gave himself and his ministers a substantial raise, Manitoba acquired a new political personality. An ex-miner and merchant from Thompson named Joe Borowski decided to camp in protest on the steps of the Legislature for two months of media coverage, official harassment and public attention before his sick wife summoned him home.

On August 6th, 1966, it was British Columbia's turn. Shrewdly, Bennett calculated that his opponents would find great difficulty in rousing voters from mid-summer torpor and he was right. However, when he began to denounce his understrength opposition for "obstructionism," he began to sound too much like a ranting dictator even for easy-going British Columbians. A Social Credit victory might be a foregone conclusion but fair play demanded at least a bit of criticism. Robert Strachan and

Tommy Douglas, their Liberal rivals and even the veteran newspaper editor, "Ma" Murray from Lilooet, roared into action against the arrogant premier and his "steamroller." Their protests came late — perhaps too late for any but the media-sensitive lower mainland to be affected — but they gave added push to a number of constituency campaigns. On September 12th, the NDP lost a few seats in the hinterland but more than made up for them in the Vancouver area and collected thirty-four per cent of the popular vote, about as much as the CCF had ever won. Among the members of the enlarged caucus was Tom Berger, an able young lawyer who had briefly represented Vancouver-Burrard in Ottawa in 1962-63.

In neighbouring Alberta, the NDP had been shut out federally and provincially since its foundation. Even there the party experienced a brief triumph. In a by-election on October 6th in the coal-mining constituency of Pincher Creek-Crowsnest, Garth Turcott, a local lawyer, unexpectedly won a seat for the party. In the provincial legislature, however, he abruptly broke the clubhouse rules by demanding that two prominent Social Credit ministers, E. W. Hinman and A. J. Hooke, answer charges already published in a Calgary newspaper. Even the vestigial Liberal and Conservative opposition rose in outrage. In the ensuing general election, Turcott found his margin erased and both he and his party were pursued through the courts for their temerity.

Though Manitoba and British Columbia were important and even a small victory in Alberta was delightful, the main contests of the second round were in Saskatchewan and Ontario. Normally, Saskatchewan would have waited until the spring of 1968 but Ross Thatcher discovered that, while the current crops were far better than expected, the economic prospects were discouraging. It was election weather. Accordingly, on September 8th, 1967, he announced that he needed a mandate to prove to investors that socialism had been banished forever. For its part, the CCF-NDP announced that it would fight the election on the sell-out of natural resources, on its policies of a new, citizen-owned development corporation and of the gradual elimination of university tuition fees.

Whatever their proposals, both parties were essentially fighting on their record and, as Dalton Camp has pointed out, a party in its first term is remarkably hard to defeat. Its predecessor's sins are not forgotten; its own novelty has not worn off. Woodrow Lloyd's denunciation of a resource sellout, however amply backed by statistics, found little favour among those who had found new jobs in the potash and oil industry or among those who were now persuaded that Saskatchewan could at last share the wealth of neighbouring Alberta. Moreover, in opposition, the CCF-NDP had behaved too much like the father of the prodigal son, prepared to welcome voters back to the same old leaders and the same old policies as soon as they had repented of their three-year folly.

In fact, the results were very close. On October 11th, the CCF-NDP collected 44.4 per cent of the vote, a better share than in any election since 1956 but, thanks to the near-disappearance of Conservative candidates, the Liberal vote rose to 45.6 per cent. Because of the province's custom of politically motivated redistribution, a sin shared by CCF and Liberal governments alike, the Liberals took thirty-five seats to the CCF-NDP's twenty-four — an election night survey suggested that it took 800 more votes to elect a CCF candidate than a Liberal and in Saskatoon, where the CCF had a city-wide majority of 1000, the Liberals took three of the five seats.

Post-election calculations and rationalizations do not win governments. True to custom, the party's ensuing convention blamed opponents and the media for the setback; it also reconfirmed Lloyd as its leader. There was only one permanent casualty — the letters CCF. Henceforth, the convention decided, the democratic Left in Saskatchewan would campaign as the New Democratic Party.

There were rumours that Thatcher had timed his election to prevent intervention by the NDP's travelling corps of organizers. During his election, they were fully engaged in Ontario. There, a new zeal for organization had produced almost 25,000 members and an annual income of $125,000 by the eve of the 1967 election. With help from unions and individuals, the organization staff had grown to thirteen and the provincial office had three full-time officers. The party's federal secretary, Terry Grier, had resigned to work with the Ontario leader, Donald MacDonald. The new provincial secretary, John Harney, a former university professor and Trevor Lloyd, a University of Toronto historian, had helped develop a party programme which stressed what they called "pragmatic radicalism." Though nominalists had been delighted by occasional references to "socialism," the *Globe and Mail* commented that the programme's emphasis on the protection of the individual from the abuses of government and corporate power might make it welcome to many conservatives. Certainly it helped attract the most impressive slate of provincial candidates the party had ever offered.

Some of the political sophistication which Grier had pioneered in the federal party came with him to Ontario. Following the federal NDP example, the party commissioned a pre-election survey — though it economized by having the analysis performed by sympathetic academics. It showed the NDP running third, but indicated that there was a significant target group of potential supporters who wanted to hear the party talk about bread and butter issues like housing and taxes rather than more esoteric interests like pollution and foreign ownership. Though MacDonald and the party leaders used the slogan "67 seats in '67," the party had, in fact, selected thirty-five constituencies for priority campaigning, doing its best to develop Riverdale-style organizations in each of them. To run the campaign, the party budgeted an unprecedented $90,000 for its central campaign, including $50,000 for an advertising campaign to be run by the Dunsky agency.

The campaign was closely related to the available political pressures. On the whole, Ontario seemed remarkably content in 1967, its only visible diseases the consequences of unplanned prosperity. However, the province's trade unionists were increasingly indignant about the use of injunctions to break strikes. After a series of defiances which left twenty-six of its members facing jail sentences, the labour movement was even more eager to attempt political action. In Sudbury, the end of inter-union battling allowed the huge Inco local, now a part of the Steelworkers, to affiliate most of its 15,000 members. In June of 1967, the NDP demonstrated the power of its new alliance by taking Sudbury from the Liberals in a bitterly-fought federal by-election. Closer to provincial concerns, the Robarts government fired its outspoken chief coroner for Toronto, Dr. Morton Shulman, and turned him into an NDP candidate.

These were not, of course, the issues which could defeat a well-established government, full of the good works and the euphoria of Centennial year, generous with promised bounty and well-supplied with money to pay for it. The Ontario Liberals, under their fourth leader since 1963, plagued by defeatism and the blunders of their federal government colleagues, were no threat. The NDP, with only eight seats as a base, could hardly dream of becoming the government. Nor did it expect to. Travelling in the unaccustomed comfort of a campaign bus, Donald Mac-

Donald made his impact on the party's chosen areas of concentration, the north and the south-west, sticking doggedly to his pre-selected themes. If electioneering can ever be a rational business, the NDP had left little to chance.

Of course, electioneering can only be as rational as the electorate. Against the political skill of John Robarts and the smooth self-confidence of the Conservative machine, the opposition parties did not seem likely to make much headway. On October 17th, the NDP did not capture its thirty-five concentration ridings or even achieve its private goal of becoming Official Opposition, but its supporters still had a lot to cheer about. The only political group to gain both seats and votes, the NDP moved from sixteen to twenty-five per cent of popular support and from eight to twenty seats in a somewhat enlarged legislature. Except for those who had believed the party's own propaganda about its prospects, it was an impressive advance.

In Manitoba, British Columbia and Ontario, the second provincial round had strengthened the NDP caucuses, rejuvenated its leadership and established the party as a credible contender for provincial power. By the end of 1967, the New Democrats could afford to be in a bullish mood.

David Lewis. In the CCF, the word was "Clear it with David." In the NDP, his ideas and his personality were even more dominant. Could anyone else replace T. C. Douglas as the party's national leader? (Julien Lebourdais) ▷

The "bearpit" session at the 1971 leadership convention. The candidates (on platforms) from the left: Frank Howard (back to the camera), Ed Broadbent, David Lewis, John Harney and James Laxer. (Federal NDP) ▽

V. Conflict

The fourth biennial convention of the NDP met in the Royal York Hotel in Toronto from July 3rd to 6th, 1967. Original plans to go to Montreal were scrapped when Expo 67 proved too expensive a competitor for hotel rooms, and there was an air of tired ritual as delegates assembled in the big, familiar, slightly shabby hotel. Perhaps in an attempt to give the gathering added excitement, Stephen Lewis, an Ontario provincial member and the eldest son of David Lewis, proclaimed that it would be a watershed for the NDP, witnessing "the emergence of a new generation socialist who is beginning to say things that people in this society are very much looking for."

That year, as both Liberals and Tories got ready to change leaders, youth was very much in fashion in Canadian politics but, if a new generation was present at the Toronto convention, it was more seen than heard. Its only coup, organized largely by the former federal secretary, Terry Grier, Grant Notley, a future Alberta leader, John Brewin, the son of a veteran M.P., John Harney, the Ontario secretary and John Penner, a prominent Montreal New Democrat, was to topple the federal officers' chosen candidate for party president. A respected ex-cabinet minister from Saskatchewan, J. H. Brockelbank's only fault was his age. Aware that the NDP would soon have the oldest leader in federal politics, the so-called "young Turks" were determined to add at least one younger face to the party hierarchy. Rebuffed by Robert Cliche and Charles Taylor, they turned to James Renwick, the victor of Riverdale. By dint of feverish canvassing, they won.

A much more important convention decision was the adoption of an extensive statement on economic planning and foreign ownership, the joint work of Max Saltsman, the M.P. from Waterloo South, and Colin Cameron, the veteran socialist M.P. from Nanaimo. The product of lengthy study, the document eschewed much of the anti-Americanism of the party's earlier (and subsequent) declarations — why blame the Americans, demanded Saltsman, "for what is essentially our own fault?" — and offered a detailed, comprehensive and wide-ranging review of what Canadians could do about their branch plant economy. In summary, it proposed mechanisms to generate domestic capital, to organize Canada's own capacity for technological innovation and to ensure that both domestic and foreign-controlled corporations served the national interest.

Of course, the 861 delegates had other interests — from passing the usual statements of concern about agriculture, women, consumers, labour and Vietnam, to listening to guest speakers. Among them was Claude Ryan, the editor of *Le Devoir*, and he brought solemn advice. Already, he claimed, the NDP had support from French Canadian union leaders and academics. Now it must turn to middle class nationalists and to the under-privileged. "Offer specific, practical solutions and Quebec will listen."

Although Ryan made no acknowledgement, the convention had already endorsed a specific constitutional solution which his own newspaper was currently urging:

"special status." It was the logical outcome of six years of resolutions and it had already been expressed in the NDP's 1965 election platform. If the party believed that the other nine provinces neither wanted nor deserved the kind of autonomy Quebec increasingly demanded, why not recognize the historical fact that she was "not a province like the others." Already the federal Liberals had offered a specific example by allowing both a Canada and a Quebec Pension Plan. As usual, it was Charles Taylor, after interminable drafting sessions, who put the words together: "In fields of government which touch a community's way of life — fields such as social security, town planning, education and community development — Quebec must have the right and the fiscal resources to adopt its own programmes and policies in place of those designed by and financed by the federal government. At the same time, the federal government must be able to play an increased role in these fields where this is desired by the people of other provinces." Once Taylor had described the formula, an even more persuasive figure, Laurier LaPierre, a McGill University historian and former popular co-host of a CBC television programme, was available to sell it to the delegates. With a little outspoken grumbling from Robert Strachan, the British Columbia leader, LaPierre, Cliche and Taylor won an overwhelming vote of support.

As a whole, the convention brought little enthusiasm from the press or the delegates. The *Financial Times* noted acidly that while the party had "peeled off yards of discarded socialist dogma," it had left "a figure as emaciated and indeterminate as Twiggy." However, on its "special status" proposal, there was a sudden, strong and, to most New Democrats, a surprisingly hostile reaction. So far, apart from some academic grumbles and the resignation of Dr. Eugene Forsey because of the "two nations" position, the NDP had suffered very little for its attempt to respond to Quebec nationalist demands. In the summer of 1967, that immunity ended. Perhaps it was President de Gaulle's outburst in Montreal, perhaps it was the uproar over the Conservatives' flirting with their own "two-nations" policy, perhaps it was a belated realization, particularly in academic circles, that separatism had become a serious force in Quebec, but suddenly it was no longer possible for the NDP to continue its good-natured attempts to find out what French Canada wanted. Ramsay Cook, a well-known historian and former NDP sympathiser, broke openly with the party on "special status," insisting that it not only opened the way to national dissolution, it also would rob English-speaking provinces of their rights. His criticisms were echoed by Kenneth McNaught, the biographer of J. S. Woodsworth. Donald Smiley, a prominent political scientist at the University of British Columbia, insisted that the NDP had practically destroyed its usefulness even by espousing the "two nations" position, "a formulation which is inherently destructive of Confederation and which is neither understood nor accepted among those groups or in most of those areas who have for a generation supported the democratic left."

Perhaps surprisingly, the party did not really answer these criticisms by pointing to the impressive historical precedents for treating Quebec differently, or emphasizing the limited realm in which the doctrine would operate. The NDP might have mobilized the frustration of Canada by arguing that the federal role throughout the country dwindled at the behest of a single region, and that a potentially far more destructive regionalism was fostered by the status quo. Instead, the party's academics retired to their studies and its parliamentary spokesmen returned to the economic and social issues which were their natural preoccupations. The party's administrators had their own problems. The new federal secretary, Clifford Scotton, transferred from the Canadian Labour Congress where he had edited its prize-winning magazine, discovered that he had acquired a substantial debt and a budget which stubbornly refused to balance. The party's financial dependence on its provincial sections meant troubles when those provinces were preoccupied with their own contests and paying the resulting debts. Even with 70,000 regular members and 245,000 more in affiliated organizations, a new record, the NDP had not escaped chronic poverty. The result was elimination of an apparently ineffective women's department and of the federal party's organization staff. Both responsibilities would fall directly on the provinces. After two years of supporting the minority Pearson government, constantly worrying about impending elections and its own financial and policy problems, the NDP was in the psychological doldrums. Perhaps in desperation, the party's federal council accepted a scheme from Laurier LaPierrre, its newest vice-president, for an "Operation New Canada — Refaire le Canada." Instead of churning its own soul for answers, the party would send out its renowned army of canvassers door-to-door "to establish the real problems Canadians have in common as well as those reflected by regional factors." The scheme never got off the ground.

Few politically-minded Canadians would have much attention to spare for the NDP and its canvassers that year. Amidst the excitement of Centennial celebrations and Expo '67 came the agony of the Conservative party's struggle to replace John Diefenbaker. By March 1967, the party's public esteem had fallen so low that the NDP actually pulled ahead of it in the Gallup polls: twenty-eight per cent to twenty-five. However, once the Tories had chosen Robert Stanfield, the tall, craggy, cautious premier of Nova Scotia, their fortunes bounded. Freshly transfixed by issues of political leadership and personality, Canadians greeted the new Conservative leader by indicating forty-two per cent support in October, enough to give the Tories a comfortable majority if Mr. Pearson had generously called an election. Instead, on December 14th, the Liberal leader announced his own impending retirement. By April, 1968, not only were there nine candidates in the race for the succession but the Liberals had recovered their commanding lead in the opinion polls. In the home stretch of the leadership race, veteran politicians were outpaced by the political novice who had voted NDP in 1963 and who had only entered Parliament in 1965. Within three weeks of his April 6th convention victory, Pierre-Elliott Trudeau dissolved parliament and presented Canadians with their twenty-eighth and, in some respects, their most extraordinary federal general election.

If Mr. Trudeau had been a more conventional as well as perhaps a more sincere reformer, he might have used his initial months in power to cleanse the party he had so often condemned, reinforcing the progressive wing in his cabinet and using his new prestige to pass a raft of overdue measures of social justice which voters could have judged in the autumn. Instead, he presented himself to the voters before the momentum and glamour of his leadership victory had been exhausted. To Conservatives, he might be the crypto-communist who had visited Cuba and Red China; to New Democrats, he was the man who had let them down in 1965 and who had emerged as an arrogant intellectual whose attitude to welfare reforms had been summed up as "no more free stuff." To most Canadians, he was virtually unknown save as the French Canadian who had successfully bullied Quebec's Premier Daniel Johnson at a televised constitutional conference. To radical liberals, he was the man who had legalized homosexuality and reportedly wished to chase the state from the bedrooms of the nation. In an extended period in Parliament, the opposition parties might have had a chance to compel the new prime minister to reveal himself and his ideas; in an election campaign, inter-party confrontation virtually ceases or is reduced to the almost meaningless and monotonous formula of a television debate or an all-candidates' meeting. The task of probing a politician falls to the news media and, in 1968, with few exceptions, its leading figures were enjoying a love affair with the new Liberal leader. Only by the end of the campaign did a few of the more perceptive of them conclude that they had been victims of a confidence trick and, even then, like most such victims, they grimaced at their own naiveté and passed on.

Though the NDP had been sending itself readiness warnings since the day after the 1965 election, and though it had momentarily expected an election in February when the Liberal government was defeated in Parliament, it was by no means anticipating the kind of campaign it faced in the spring of 1968. In some respects, of course, it was ready. Two and a half years had been time to collect an array of attractive new candidates and the prospect of a post-election leadership change drew others into the race. Douglas Fisher chose to run in Toronto's sprawling York Centre; John Harney, the Ontario NDP secretary, ran in a new riding of Scarborough West; Bruce Rogers, a widely-known CBC announcer, was nominated in Toronto-Parkdale. In Montreal, Laurier LaPierre was the candidate in suburban Lachine. Already, *Maclean's Magazine* had tipped him as the first socialist prime minister of Canada. In Dollard, Charles Taylor had built an organization and, at Quebec NDP insistence, Robert Cliche had retreated from Beauce to find a seat in working class Duvernay, an area which had done well for the party in 1965. In other respects, the party was caught at a disadvantage. Money was short. Party prospects, bright in 1967 and even in early 1968, had sagged. Party leaders were exhausted and the party's message, fundamentally unchanged since 1961, seemed tiresomely familiar. Advertising arrangements already made with the Dunsky agency were recalled, amended and re-established with little alteration after the campaign had started, involving a significant loss of time and money.

The party's approach to the election conveyed honesty or lack of confidence according to viewpoint. In earlier campaigns, Douglas felt that he had damaged his credibility by telling the truth about everything but the party's prospects which, true to established custom, he wildly exaggerated. In 1968, he began by confessing that the party could not win but that it had designs on capturing fifty seats. It happened to be the truth but there was a chorus of anguish from party regulars and of ridicule from the news media. By the end of the campaign, buoyed up by evidence that the party was fighting a more effective and well-organized campaign than even it had expected, Douglas was willing to increase his estimate from 50 to 132 seats. The party's campaign slogan, "You win when you vote NDP," also reflected realism (or defeatism) with its argument against those who complained about "losing their votes" by backing candidates who could not win or form part of a government. In the NDP view, you lost your vote only when you voted against your own interests, and for ordinary working people, concerned about issues which the NDP saw as important, like jobs, homes, taxes and the cost of living, that meant voting Liberal or Conservative.

Douglas's own campaign was based on the need to bring the dashing, romantic Liberal leader to bay on crucial economic issues. Of these, the most important had become foreign ownership, reflected in the report of the Watkins task force, and tax reform, advocated by the massive report of the Carter Royal Commission. The NDP had extensive policies to capture any interest in economic nationalism, and Douglas propounded them from coast to coast, including branch-plant centres like Windsor and Toronto. Constantly, he hammered Trudeau, the professed anti-nationalist, and his party, as committed to a policy of continentalism. Except in a national television debate between the three English-speaking leaders, in which Douglas scored so heavily that the media began again to take the NDP seriously, the party had simply no means of forcing the Liberals to their ground.

Only on one issue did the two parties meet head-on: Quebec. If Trudeau promised anything beyond charisma and what Britain's Harold Wilson had called "the smack of firm government," it was an end of concessions to Quebec nationalists. For the first time, NDP candidates began to be confronted with the issue in the rest of Canada. In Douglas's new riding (redistribution had disintegrated the faithful Burnaby-Coquitlam), his opponent was the former provincial Liberal leader, an able campaigner who portrayed the NDP leader as the spokesman for a remote, alien and aggressive Quebec. Ramsay Cook, the former NDP supporter, rode prominently in Trudeau's entourage. In Quebec, hopes were high. The new prime minister's defiance of the nationalists brought the NDP support from unfamiliar places, including two ministers in the Union Nationale government, Gabriel Loubier and Paul Allard. Organizers, including two of Ontario's ablest constituency specialists, Stephen Lewis and Gerald Caplan, were sent to help Taylor, Cliche and other key candidates. However, the seemingly fatal misfortunes which beset the NDP's ventures in French Canada struck again. While the press made what they could of alleged differences between Douglas and Cliche, the Liberals persuaded Eric Kierans, a

respected and progressive Montreal Liberal and an unsuc-
cessful rival of Trudeau for his party's leadership, to run
for Duvernay.

NDP campaign lore suggests that Conservative voters are
usually visible and audible; it is Liberals at the doorstep
who are smilingly noncommittal. By the eve of June 25th,
one could build high hopes on the basis of apparent NDP
support but veteran campaigners counted the uncom-
mitted and worried. Then came St-Jean Baptiste day. The
eve-of-election broadcasts of the prime minister calmly
defying separatist rioters helped spur weakly motivated
Liberal voters to the polls, saving their party from most of
the customary slump between final Gallup estimates and
the real thing. It certainly did no harm. The Trudeau
campaign took 45.2 per cent of the popular vote and an
eventual 155 seats, more than enough for a comfortable
majority. For the NDP, spirits belatedly raised by a surge
of volunteers, apparent support and Douglas's performance, it was a bitter defeat. Every one of the
apparently potential national leaders – Taylor, LaPierre,
Harney, Fisher – was defeated. Across northern Ontario,
the NDP lost three of its four seats as Franco-Ontarian
voters swung back to Liberalism. It was even worse in
British Columbia where the party's vote slumped below
the Liberals for the first time since 1963. With redistribution, the party should have taken eleven seats; it lost
four of them and, worst of all, one of them belonged to
Tommy Douglas. In Montreal, where Duvernay was almost
the only serious contest, Robert Cliche joined him in
defeat.

For those who sought comfort from the NDP result, it
could be found. Losses in Ontario and British Columbia
had been handsomely compensated by gains in Saskatchewan where the party had gained thousands of voters
who had stayed with Diefenbaker since 1957 or 1958. For

the first time since Argue's defection, the party had representation in the prairie province — six M.P.s and a by-election would eventually add a seventh. Across Canada, the party's total vote was 1,390,221, 17.4 per cent of the total and an answer to those who had claimed in 1965 that the party's support was merely a protest vote. In the industrial areas and in most of the major cities, the NDP had lost ground but it had kept its position as the alternative.

If the new parliament had been one of minorities, faced with yet another imminent election, the NDP would doubtless have pulled itself together, counted its blessings, exaggerated them a little, and soldiered on. With the new House of Commons firmly in place until 1972 or even later, there was no need. The party could abandon itself to its sorrows. Deprived of many of its leaders, bruisingly reminded that it had again been brought to an electoral standstill, the party found that it had accumulated a debt of over a hundred thousand dollars. By the end of 1968, its central newspaper had been scrapped and its research department dissolved — to be re-established under federal caucus control as a result of sudden new government benevolence to opposition parties. It was a more serious loss than the party could immediately realize for it was a sacrifice of its only internal mechanism for policy gene-ration and innovation. Henceforth, caucus research direc-tors were to play a part in NDP policy review but their primary focus would inevitably be on the day-to-day preoccupations of Parliament. As the party turned to self-examination in the months and years after the 1968 election, the absence of a clear, uncluttered lead from the party's own internal resources would leave an intellectual vacuum.

In the immediate aftermath of the 1968 election, leadership seemed a more salient question than policy. For

years, the Canadian news media had had a fixation about
political leadership, first in the controversial figure of John
Diefenbaker, now in the person of Pierre-Elliott Trudeau.
The NDP had not been immune. Immediately before the
1968 campaign was launched, Stephen Lewis had flown to
Vancouver to persuade Tommy Douglas that he should
clear the way for a new leader. Certainly, responded
Douglas, he was no Diefenbaker. He would stay no longer
than his party wished, but he also felt that the replacement
must come from a new generation. Lewis's father, narrowly re-elected in York South and soon to be chosen as
NDP house leader, would hardly qualify. Who would? Ed
Schreyer, the thirty-two year old M.P. from Selkirk,
apparently yearned to return to Manitoba politics.
Winnipeg's Stanley Knowles and Andrew Brewin, the M.P.
for Toronto-Greenwood and NDP foreign affairs critic, were
both veteran CCFers. Taylor, LaPierre, Harney, Fisher and
other hopefuls had all been defeated and Ed Broadbent, a
young York University political scientist who had just
been elected from Oshawa-Whitby, was utterly untried.
Taylor, young, bilingual, attractive and articulate in a
slightly academic way, was the favourite of the party
leaders, but he was reluctant to consider himself a
candidate and adamant that he would not seek a seat
outside Quebec. At an executive meeting immediately
after the 1968 election, Douglas announced his intention
to step down at the 1969 convention, and repeated this to
press reporters. A statement was issued from the meeting
to this effect. Then, at the urging of the party council,
Douglas remained, accepting an assignment to study the
NDP's electoral methods. That chore was promptly forgotten when Colin Cameron, re-elected for Nanaimo-
Cowichan-The Islands, suddenly died. His seat, by no
means safe but among the best at the party's disposal, was
available and Douglas headed west for his sixth personal

battle for a place in Parliament since he had come back to federal politics.

The problem of leadership was not merely federal. In 1968, most of the party's provincial leaders — Strachan in British Columbia, Lloyd in Saskatchewan, Paulley in Manitoba and MacDonald in Ontario — had also been CCF leaders. Of course, as the NDP had boasted during the Diefenbaker shambles, their leaders had to win approval at every party convention but, as Robert Michels pointed out in his classic study of the German Social Democrats, left-wing parties are more prone to criticize their leaders than replace them. To them, ideology rather than personality should be the salient feature of political decision-making. It had always seemed unfair to blame a leader when it was the party's policies and image which clearly barred it at the polls. Moreover, both the CCF and the NDP made such extortionate demands on the time, energy and financial security of their leaders that it seemed common decency to leave them in the quiet enjoyment of whatever meagre pleasures the office afforded. Except for Argue, the CCF leadership had been held by only Woodsworth and Coldwell. In Ontario, MacDonald was only the second person to hold the CCF or NDP leadership.

That era of tolerance was fading. In 1967, Tom Berger, elected to the British Columbia legislature only a year before, challenged Robert Strachan. The result was a bruising contest which pitted the party's provincial office against the majority of the caucus and split the party into a more radical old guard and a more pragmatic group of "young Turks." Strachan won but the bitterness was sufficiently sustained that the party found it prudent to bring organizers from Ontario to help run Douglas's Nanaimo by-election campaign and to share in the victory.

A year later, both Paulley and MacDonald faced similar

tests. The Manitoba leader's ill-health and his limited
appeal to ethnic and middle-class voters persuaded another
relative newcomer, Sidney Green, a Winnipeg lawyer and
former municipal councillor, to make his bid. By making it
clear that he was simply keeping his seat warm for the
popular Ed Schreyer, Paulley kept his job but only by 213
votes to 168. In Ontario, where Donald MacDonald had
been shepherding the CCF-NDP back from near annihilation since 1953, there could be no question of strength
and ability, only a claim that he had acquired a "loser's
image." The challenge came from James Renwick, the
party's federal president, with the argument that the
party's significant advance in the 1967 election was a
setback, not a triumph, and that MacDonald had to bear
the responsibility. Backed by Stephen Lewis and a
minority in the provincial caucus, Renwick began his
campaign by insisting that his cool image would attract
more of Ontario's traditionally conservative voters than
MacDonald's. At the convention, he switched images, with
an appeal to the party's radical wing. With almost thirteen
hundred delegates attracted to Kitchener for the unwonted
excitement, MacDonald won by a margin of 859 to 370.

At the federal level, too, change of leadership was
postponed, not least by the conclusion that it would be
too expensive. To make a leadership convention sufficiently democratic, the party would have to help
delegates from more remote provinces with their travel
expenses and that, the heavily indebted party was not in a
position to do. Instead, the party announced that its 1969
convention in Winnipeg would concentrate on policy. "In
our preoccupation with the mechanisms of elections," a
party newsletter observed, "we have had to forego the
thorough and continuing review of philosophy and program which should characterize democratic socialist
parties."

Constitutionally, policy-making in the NDP starts with the resolutions which constituency associations and affiliated organizations submit to conventions and councils. These are solemnly translated, printed and distributed in their hundreds to delegates. Unfortunately, it is rare to find among the submitted resolutions any which sufficiently encapsulate a party stand on the more complex and current of political issues. In some cases, a workable composite could be assembled from a number of grassroots resolutions; more often, in the CCF and the NDP, it was customary for the party's research or policy review committee or even a convention resolutions committee to draft a statement for submission under the auspices of the party's council. That was how the NDP had evolved its policies on federalism, foreign ownership and a host of more mundane matters. It was a process which depended on a fair degree of consensus within the party about its policies and a reasonable degree of confidence in its leaders. During the Sixties, much of the work was done by Taylor, George Cadbury, the party's treasurer and a committed British socialist, Marion Bryden, the Ontario party's research director, and J. C. Weldon, an economist at McGill, together with a succession of federal party research directors.

In the aftermath of the 1968 election, by its own definition of the term, the NDP turned "left." In part, this was because of a premature judgement that Trudeau, himself, represented a leftward lunge by the Liberal party. Certainly middle class radicals had been enchanted by what seemed to be his view of external affairs, private morality and "participatory democracy." To a degree the NDP was slow to appreciate, its own working class base had been remarkably immune from Trudeaumania but the party's middle class supporters had been badly singed by it. Outside Canada, there were other pressures. United

States involvement in Vietnam seemed a travesty of the ideals of liberal internationalism and produced, particularly among American intellectual opinion leaders, a remorseless critique of their own flawed society. In Britain, the failure of Harold Wilson's Labour government to solve the country's economic problems devalued the most important single source of NDP ideas and political philosophy. Within Canadian politics, most of the content of the NDP's faded green programme book seemed to have been expended. National medicare was due on July 1st, 1969. Canada had a national portable pension plan, departments for regional development and manpower planning and, under Trudeau, she would soon even recognize the People's Republic of China. Certainly the NDP could insist that all could have been done better and sooner and, more to the point, that critical elements remained in the party programme, almost untouched. But it was getting more difficult to claim to the party's own radicals that the sum of all of the NDP's social democratic measures added up to their vision of a socialist society.

By the late Sixties, it was increasingly fashionable to talk of a rejection of established politics, particularly by the young. Editorial writers expended quantities of their own wisdom and of their publishers' ink on the prospect. In May of 1968, Paris had been paralyzed by student riots and in the United States and Canada, civil rights, student and Quebec nationalist demonstrators began to abandon non-violence in an almost atavistic enthusiasm for destruction. Everywhere these outbursts were the work of small minorities; almost everywhere they were ineffectual. The French government went on much as before. In Canada, the young flocked to Trudeau as they would four years later. Revolutionary protest produced a flow of comfortable jobs for the children of the middle class and radical chic became an aphrodisiac for their elders. The NDP could not possibly have remained immune. For a party which had not been dramatically successful at the ballot box, there were many who now insisted that the choice was either oblivion or surging into the streets.

Pressures for a more radical NDP began at the top. In December, 1968, David Lewis persuaded most of the federal caucus to spend a week-end at Wakefield in the Gatineau hills, listening to papers by Charles Taylor, exploring the extent of corporate power, and Kari Levitt, a radical McGill economist, analyzing the implications of the branch-plant economy on Canadian economic and even political independence. Later that winter, amidst obvious uneasiness from the party's leading trade unionists, Ed Broadbent started an enthusiastic study of industrial democracy. In a process launched by Lewis, Taylor and the party's latest research director, Marc Eliesen, a substantial number of papers were soon circulating on topics ranging from guaranteed annual income and urbanization to science policy and sports. To ensure that party members and the public had some inkling of the development, the Ontario party published a thirty-page booklet, entitled *Socialism Canada Seventies*, summarising the papers and their general direction. "A union of awareness and experience," claimed the introduction, "has brought a radicalism to the re-definition of the New Democratic Party in the Seventies which may astonish those who believed that we were drifting into the comfortable consensus."

The public reaction, to judge from the press, was cool, if not splenetic. In two furious editorials, the Toronto *Globe & Mail* condemned the booklet and its ideas as simultaneously anti-American and anti-Canadian while Douglas Fisher, once again a columnist for the Toronto *Telegram*, suggested that its authors were the sort of theoreticians that a wise party hid at the back of the committee rooms, folding leaflets. Within the party, reaction had already been overtaken by the emergence of a group which, for the most part, had little to do with either leading party members or the traditional, Trotskyist-infiltrated Socialist Caucus. The inspiration came from James Laxer, a big, attractive and highly articulate graduate student who had inherited his politics from his father, formerly a leading Communist, and his experience from the Canadian student movement in the Sixties. He was joined by Gerald Caplan, who had run campaigns for David Lewis in the early Sixties while still a student, by Ed Broadbent, the only academic radical in the NDP federal caucus and by Mel Watkins, the University of Toronto economist whose report had been a handbook for Douglas in the 1968 campaign, but who had now moved through continentalism and liberal nationalism into a full-scale, doctrinaire socialism. In the spring of 1969, this group and others attracted to it drafted a "Manifesto for an Independent Socialist Canada." The chief authors, so far as a collective enterprise could have them, were Laxer, Broadbent and Caplan. In a phrase apparently coined by Broadbent, the document deliberately rejected concessions to consensus radicalism: if it waffled, it would "waffle to the left." Tactically, it was loaded with the rhetorical symbols which could crystallize the "left" in a party where it was increasingly wrong to be "right." Emotionally, it was a catharsis for younger, radical academics, fed up with catering to the presumed tastes of the mass electorate and eager to challenge a party leadership which had delivered neither electoral victory nor spiritual gratification.

In a paper prepared for the party's policy review committee and summarised in *Socialism Canada Seventies*, Watkins had presented part of the reasoning which lay behind the Manifesto: "On the road to socialism, aspirations for independence or feelings of nationalism and particularly anti-imperialism, should be taken into account in their own right. For to pursue independence in a serious way in Canada is to make visible the necessity and desirability of socialism." In short, an appeal to the cyclical mood of Canadian nationalism was a convenient way to recruit mass support for socialism. Although the Manifesto ranged across a broad spectrum of left-wing concerns, from women's liberation to industrial democracy, its two chief themes were a fervid anti-Americanism (the attributes of American society were characterized as "militarism abroad and racism at home") and a harkening back to the certitudes of the Regina Manifesto ("Capitalism must be replaced by socialism, by national planning of investment and by public ownership of the means of production in the interests of the Canadian people as a whole.").

The argument was not universally accepted. Although Donald Creighton, Canada's most Tory historian, allegedly gave his blessing to the Waffle cause, George Bain, then the *Globe and Mail's* perceptive Ottawa columnist, wondered whether, if socialism was the price of independence, Canadians might not reject both. A colleague of Watkins, Abraham Rotstein, who had exercised a powerful influence on both the NDP and Watkins in the direction of economic nationalism, was obviously dismayed that his views had been trapped in an out-dated brand of socialism. Like Cameron and Saltsman in their 1967 paper, which Rotstein had certainly influenced, he insisted that the NDP had a wide range of mechanisms to counter the effects of external economic domination. However, neither these nor other criticisms of style or text could persuade the authors to modify their Manifesto. Intransigence cost them the support of Charles Taylor and of Ed Broadbent, their only M.P. and a part-author, but it did not deter a total of ninety-four signatories, most of them academics, and including Laurier LaPierre, Cy Gonick, the Winnipeg editor and publisher of *Canadian Dimension*, and Dave Barrett, a British Columbia M.L.A. and a recent leadership aspirant.

Ostensibly, New Democrats possess great enthusiasm for policy discussion; in fact, it is a minority taste. Robbed of the excitement of a leadership contest, the Winnipeg convention had few charms and registrations lagged until the emergence of the Manifesto brought promise of a major battle. In retrospect, the party leaders might have been wiser to accept the Manifesto, grit their teeth during the ensuing storm and trust that it would fall into the capacious oblivion reserved for the party's prose. But like most outsiders, including columnists Doug Fisher and Harry Crowe, they under-estimated the support the Manifesto would draw and, like Broadbent and Taylor, they soon discovered the utter inflexibility of its architects. Hurriedly, David Lewis and Taylor drafted an alternative statement, "For a United and Independent Canada," restating the theme of economic and political nationalism in more familiar NDP language, and won endorsement by the party's federal council prior to the convention on October 25th.

The ensuing four days were a nightmare for party regulars. To democratise procedures, the party had adopted a "panel" structure for the convention, allowing simultaneous debate on resolutions, more participation and greater productivity than in the more familiar plenary sessions. A procedural loophole allowed the Left to rush its forces from panel to panel for crucial votes. It took a couple of days before the moderates were sufficiently organized to counter-attack but soon rival clutches of delegates were sent panting through the corridors of Winnipeg's vast Civic Auditorium. Next, the Left cried foul play when the majority overthrew most of their victories during the ratifying plenary sessions. The Left's chief triumph was the NDP's final abandonment of support for NATO. The convention highlight was an hour-long, nationally-televised debate between supporters of the rival manifestos. Teams of speakers, including most of the potential federal leadership aspirants, followed Watkins and Lewis to separate microphones. When the television coverage and a good many more pedestrian speeches had ended, a fair number of the delegates had departed, but enough remained to endorse the Lewis-Taylor document by 499 votes to 268.

The critical moment of the Waffle movement came not with the production of the manifesto but at the end of the convention. Collectively, the NDP had responded to the left-wing pressure as any party would, by co-option and concession. Watkins was elected a party vice-president; seven of the twenty party councillors elected by the convention were prominent Waffle backers. The "United Canada" statement, while closer to the NDP mainstream, had swung considerably to the left of previous party policy. The articulate, youthful leaders of the Waffle had acquired considerable respect from the party and a good many voted against their document less from conviction than because it was "bad politics." In the convention aftermath, the Wafflers were in an influential position to contribute their own current to the party's mainstream.

That was not the New Left style. In the jargon of the student movement, in which some of its leaders had learned their politics, Waffle demands on the NDP were "non-negotiable." They were also automatically escalating. Later, both Watkins and Laxer confessed astonishment at the level of support they obtained at Winnipeg. After four days of meeting, plotting, mutual congratulation and media attention, what was the point of stopping? Youthful adherents, assured by the media that their role was confrontation with their elders, decided to act out their parts. Veteran CCFers, unreconciled to the New Party broadening out, sensed that the party might be shoved back to its old moorings. Even NDP activists could escape from the frustrations of a near-decade of electoral politics by becoming part of a morally fulfilling movement.

In a paradox Wafflers could hardly appreciate, because of a cultural and intellectual continentalism few of them could even perceive, the Waffle was pressing the NDP to follow the route of the American Left. In the late 1960s, with ghetto and university riots, Vietnam demonstrations and an entire country in a state of turbulence, it seemed a fashionable and widely publicised route. Radical chic obscured the fact that taking to the streets is a tactic of the weak. The Waffle demands on the NDP echoed, almost unconsciously, those of the American New Left, from the rhetoric of "American imperialism" to appeals for sexual freedom and for the tactics of extra-parliamentary protest. To a degree, the NDP responded. A federal party committee, with Karl Jaffary, a Toronto alderman, and James Laxer as co-chairmen, was appointed to explore tactics of community organization. The Ontario party actually approved financial aid for a community action experiment in Kitchener.

To confront the NDP rather than work entirely within it required a separate organization. A newsletter was prepared, a network of "steering committees" was established, based in Toronto, and, to avoid charges of a separate membership, individuals indicated their support by joining a "mailing list." Funds were collected and, at its height, the Waffle hired organizers for its activities, maintained an office and issued statements to the press. With the news media increasingly tuned in to Canadian nationalism and naturally eager for news of intra-party dissension, Waffle leaders like Watkins and Laxer were frequent performers and their differences with the NDP leadership got regular, if *ex parte*, airing. For party leaders, the challenge of the Waffle posed a difficult and increasingly exasperating dilemma. On the one hand, the group included able, personable individuals, potential recruits for the next generation of party leaders. The Waffle had tapped a genuine need among many constituency members. It could shelter behind the party's respect for democratic dissent and its inherent anti-authoritarianism. On the other hand, particularly in the middle-class milieu where both the Waffle and the party's leadership operated, it was apparent that the NDP's position was being steadily obscured. The party's disunity was exploited in the media and by those, particularly the Conservatives, who had their own problems in that area. Most offensive to party leaders, especially in Ontario and Manitoba, was the increasing tendency by Waffle spokes-men to attack trade union leaders and, particularly, international unions. Even the original Manifesto had been restrained in that area, but Wafflers soon discovered and exploited the deep well of anti-union sentiment among both old CCFers and the young. By and large, the NDP leadership had remained restlessly quiet under attack; pro-NDP union leaders like Larry Sefton of the Steel-workers and Dennis MacDermott, the new Canadian director of the United Autoworkers, were not so tolerant. Veterans of fighting both Liberals and Communists in their own unions, they detected identical kinds of abuse from Waffle spokesmen.

Perhaps the chief problem for the NDP leadership and for many of their rank-and-file supporters in meeting the challenge was that they were too busy with the routine but unavoidable chores of running a political party between elections. Debts had to be paid off, conferences organized, government policies criticized. When neither a provincial nor a federal election loomed, there was usually a by-election campaign to be conducted. An exhausted cadre of leaders and workers had little time to spare to meet Waffle criticisms or to expound a clearer definition of the responsibilities and limitations of the New Democratic Party as an instrument for political change. A handful of pamphlets and occasional sessions at schools for election workers were insufficient to explain that the NDP did not have to follow the path of branch-plant radicalism, that it had a tradition of its own and a goal — to become a majority party of the democratic left. It was the Americans, after all, who had allowed their own socialist party to die.

VI. Progress

"While we have a responsibility as politicians to provide the public with leadership on social concerns, we're being ineffective politicians if we are so far out in front the public can't even see us."

The sentiments may have jarred on Waffle sympathisers at the 1969 convention but they came from a man most delegates had never expected to see at an NDP meeting: a New Democratic premier of Manitoba.

In 1966, when the party garnered twenty-three per cent of the provincial vote, it had reached the limits of its traditional Manitoba support. Where could it go next? A very few people thought it might try for power. Three years later, most of the familiar faces in Manitoba politics were gone. Defeated in a bid for the Tory national leadership and again in the 1968 election, Duff Roblin had retired to a Montreal boardroom. His successor, a Minnedosa funeral director named Walter Weir, scrapped Roblin's mild progressivism and returned to a familiar Manitoba preoccupation — cutting taxes. The leaderless Liberals turned to a veteran of the Fifties named Bobby Bend, whose only detectable policy was to out-Weir Weir. By 1969, the provincial government faced a number of troubles. The noisiest was Indian and environmentalist protest against a hydro development which would drown South Indian Lake; the quietest was the disturbing state of Churchill Forest Industries, a complex scheme of public and private co-operation at The Pas, launched by Roblin in 1966. Weir saw his chance. If Trudeau could win in 1968 by being rude at a federal-provincial conference, so could he. Accordingly, he went to Ottawa, pounded the table against bilingualism for the sake of the television cameras, and returned to announce a provincial election for June 25th, 1969.

Weir expected to catch the NDP leaderless. Russ Paulley had resigned at the beginning of the year and a convention was scheduled for the end of June. Instead, the date was shifted to June 7th and nominating meetings provided a setting for debates between the two contenders, Sid Green and Ed Schreyer, the thirty-three year old M.P. for Selkirk, political science lecturer and the former CCF boy wonder who had captured Brokenhead riding at the age of twenty-two. With lengthy television coverage as a bonus, Schreyer swept the convention by 506 votes to 177, leaving the impression of a cool, unflappable moderate. While Weir left his campaign to an advertising agency and the Liberals tried to pretend that the unfortunate Bend was Trudeau, Schreyer whirled through the ethnic areas of northern and eastern Manitoba, switching to German, French and Ukrainian to persuade his listeners to ignore directives from traditional leaders to stick by the Conservatives. When Weir and Bend denounced socialism, Schreyer insisted that he was a social democrat with a list of specifics: premium-free Medicare, government-run auto insurance, consolidation of Winnipeg's municipal governments, better roads for the North, more public housing. When Weir defended the South Indian Lake diversion and Bend promised to stop it, Schreyer cautiously offered a fresh study. On an even more sensitive issue in Manitoba politics, the federal government's Official Languages Act, he was unequivocal: acceptance of the Act was NDP policy.

To some ethnic leaders, that was more ammunition against the NDP; to their followers, it made less difference. Schreyer was the first non-Anglo-Saxon party leader since John Norquay in a province where other groups now totalled a significant majority. Almost imperceptibly, the NDP had broadened its ethnic representation; the others, particularly the ruling Conservatives, had not. Perhaps too, as Tom Peterson has suggested, the Schreyer campaign transcended traditional ethnic voting patterns; Manitobans stopped voting because they were French or German or Jewish and began picking parties because they favoured the rich or the poor. Meanwhile, the Manitoba party benefited from an impressive influx of organizers, among them Ontario's Terry Grier.

It may have helped a little that the experts were so unanimous. Weir would win, they promised. If there was any change, Bend might be beaten and Schreyer would lead a strong opposition. On that assumption, almost fifty years to the day after the Winnipeg General Strike collapsed, Manitobans voted. By a narrow margin, they elected the first actual New Democratic Party government in Canada. When the recounts were over, Schreyer and his candidates had collected 38.1 per cent of the votes and twenty-eight New Democrats were elected. The Conservatives, at 35.5 per cent, had elected twenty-five and the Liberals, at 23.9 per cent, had five. To complicate matters there was an Independent and a Social Crediter. Despite frenzied efforts to manufacture a "stop-the-Socialists" coalition, one Liberal, Larry Desjardins, announced that he would sit with the NDP. Schreyer's vote-losing defence of French-Canadian rights had ironically given the NDP

power. Three weeks after the election, a bitter and bewildered Weir made way for the new government.

Schreyer had inherited no prize. His majority was shaky, his caucus inexperienced and by no means dependable. It spanned the spectrum from Desjardins to Cy Gonick and back again to the unpredictable, explosive tribune of the people, Joe Borowski. Even more serious was the absence of the trained, venturesome bureaucracy which had made so many of the triumphs of the Saskatchewan CCF possible. In 1944, T. C. Douglas had been able to recruit brilliantly talented people from across Canada and in the United States and Great Britain to share the challenge of running North America's first socialist government. Who, in the summer of 1969, would abandon a well-paid career to work for a government whose life expectancy had to be counted in weeks, not months? The available civil service machinery was the product of generations of some of the most conservative and penny-pinching regimes in Canada.

In spite of the difficulties, in spite of orders from Winnipeg newspapers to consider himself merely a care-taker premier, in spite of predictions from *Canadian Dimension* that he would betray the socialist revolution he had never promised, Schreyer announced that his government would run its full term, there would be no snap election and that he would do what he had promised during the campaign. And he did. An August session of the Legislature strengthened the power of the province's proposed ombudsman, imposed a four-day cooling-off period on door-to-door sales, cut the voting age to eighteen, raised welfare allowances by ten per cent and started a series of increases in the province's minimum wage. Medicare premiums were slashed by eighty-eight per cent and the cost was transferred to income and corporation taxes. Expostulating opposition politicians struggled to find reasons to object, failed and went along.

◁ Ed Schreyer. The election of the NDP in Manitoba in 1969 was the first major breakthrough for the party since its formation. Schreyer's firm allegiance to "social democracy" offended some of the party faithful but reassured Manitoba voters. (Manitoba NDP)

When, in December, the government started to face
trouble, it was for a major element in its election platform
— government-run, universal, no-fault auto insurance.
Since 1946, Saskatchewan motorists had been saving
money from a government plan and not even the Thatcher
government had dared to cancel it. Both the CCF and the
NDP had argued that universal coverage from a single
carrier, the government, meant protection for everyone,
lower premiums and a great reduction in litigation. The
Saskatchewan plan annually proved the point. Even private
insurance agents sometimes complained that their automobile business was a source of trouble but, when
threatened by its loss, they rallied with all the impressive
power of the North American insurance industry behind
them. Schreyer and his colleagues found themselves at the
centre of the kind of barrage the Saskatchewan government had experienced during the medicare debate. Public
relations firms deployed their genius in letter-writing
campaigns, full-page newspaper advertisements and a
number of "spontaneous" demonstrations of public wrath.
Bumper stickers blossomed and the opposition joined the
fight.

In the Legislature, the government staggered. Desjardins
and some elected New Democrats began to shift under the
pressure. On April 22nd, when a government minister
announced details of the plan, the opposition pressure
built fast. A crowd of 7,000 gathered outside the
Legislature to condemn the government; in the chamber
itself, scenes verged on bedlam. The provincial NDP, by no
means strong in members or money, summoned help from
other provincial sections to produce a grassroots campaign
to counter the insurance lobby. By the end of July, when
Desjardins announced that he could not support the bill,
an election suddenly became imminent. Then, with aston-
ishing suddenness, the storm subsided. The Winnipeg

newspapers, vitriolic against the socialists, proclaimed that an election would be unwise and unnecessary. The clamor died away like magic. Schreyer, who almost alone had remained calm in the turmoil, announced a handful of concessions to individual agents who might be hurt by the government scheme. Desjardins and even an independent switched back and the bill became law.

The car insurance battle gave Manitoba almost its first political excitement in generations. It also demonstrated that the NDP government was no mere electoral accident. When the legislative session finally adjourned, even the Conservative-leaning Winnipeg *Tribune* confessed that it had been "the longest and most productive of new legislation in the history of Manitoba." Wiretapping was outlawed, hospital insurance coverage was extended to nursing homes for the elderly, and the most thorough landlord and tenant legislation in Canada was adopted, including the appointment of a "rentalsman" to help settle disputes. An election act limited campaign spending, compelled reporting of contributions and abolished the candidate deposit. Over noisy opposition from mining interests, the government forced through taxes and royalty agreements which more than doubled provincial income from mineral resources.

While Ed Schreyer wrestled with the unfamiliar problems of power, his June victory sent hopes soaring in British Columbia. There, too, the NDP found itself with a cool, moderate new leader. At the beginning of 1969, Robert Strachan had announced that he would not stand again for the leadership. A tall, dignified and eloquent carpenter from Nanaimo, he had too little appeal and too many defeats to his record for the party's middle-class backers. The organizationally-inclined complained that he limited his role to the province's brief legislative session. The struggle for the succession brought four candidates to the convention but only two, Tom Berger and Dave Barrett, an exuberant former social worker, possessed widespread support. Of the two, sober, intellectual, politically moderate Tom Berger claimed the support of union leaders, party executive, most caucus members and, by a narrow thirty-six votes, the convention.

Berger's personality and the apparent lessons of Schreyer's victory determined the campaign. If British Columbians could ever be persuaded to trust the NDP, the earnest, slightly solemn Vancouver lawyer and his slate of businessmen and professionals could surely do it. With Wally Ross and Michael Lewis, another son of David, to organize the campaign, an Ontario-style canvassing approach was attempted in constituencies where the NDP had barely ever knocked on a door. Priority ridings were selected, organizers assigned and money spent in a "now or never" mood. Berger's tour, carefully tailored to cover the party's priority areas, allowed him to lay out his programme and to insist that the party's plans for public ownership began and ended with car insurance and the British Columbia Telephone Company.

Moderation cut no ice with W. A. C. Bennett. He and his followers were as aware of the Manitoba upset as the NDP and his province would not be caught napping. When he announced the election on July 21st, taking full advantage of the summer doldrums, Bennett proclaimed that it was to meet the menace of "Marxist Socialism." The usual flood of public works was mixed with florid denunciations of Berger as "the city slicker labour lawyer" and his party as the "New Depression Party." It was a battle, insisted Bennett, between "those who seek a responsible, developing private enterprise economy and those who would impose on you the heavy hand of socialism." As usual, the message was not limited to the premier's booming voice but echoed across billboards, full-page advertisements, a crescendo of television spots and even a government-financed film. On August 27th, the Berger approach was tested — and it failed. The NDP vote, 33.9 per cent, was almost as high a share as the Left had known in the province but Social Credit support reached a new record, 46.8 per cent. The Liberals, safe in their middle-class strongholds, were untouched but the NDP lost five seats, including Berger's own. "The people of British Columbia have stopped the Socialists in their tracks," exulted Bennett, adding the somewhat Delphic comment that, perhaps, there would not need to be any more elections. He was, he explained to reporters, "plugged into God."

Berger, obviously, was not. Within weeks, he had abandoned the NDP leadership and returned to his neglected law practice. Whatever his political resemblance to Schreyer, British Columbia was not Manitoba and Bennett was distinctly not Walter Weir. Berger's inevitable successor was Dave Barrett. Flamboyant, rhetorically radical, extroverted, he made few efforts to conciliate traditional factions in the party and almost no overtures to the province's trade union leaders. Laden with debt and damaged by the failure of a campaign on which it had staked so much, the provincial organization sagged close to collapse. The party's office in Vancouver was almost closed for lack of funds. In the circumstances, it hardly seemed to matter who led the British Columbia NDP.

That was not true in Ontario or Saskatchewan and in 1970 both provincial sections changed leader. After the Winnipeg convention, the left wing had returned to Saskatchewan with sufficient momentum to dominate the provincial convention and sweep most of the executive positions. To the dismay of Woodrow Lloyd, the most prominent party leader to support the Waffle Manifesto, members of his provincial caucus and moderate leaders set to work to regain control. Combined with growing doubts of his ability to lead the party back to power and his own deteriorating health, this was enough to persuade the provincial leader to announce that he would not seek re-election in 1970. After efforts to persuade him to reconsider failed, by mid-April a first candidate was in the field; Allan Blakeney, a fortyish Regina lawyer, former Rhodes Scholar from Nova Scotia and a respected minister in the CCF-NDP governments. By July 2nd, when the convention opened in the Regina Armouries, there were three more — Roy Romanow, a Saskatoon lawyer and MLA, clearly on the right; Don Mitchell, the Waffle nominee, and George Taylor, a Saskatoon lawyer and alderman whose ideological position lay somewhere between those of Mitchell and Blakeney. With candidates and their supporters scrambling for votes, both moderates and Wafflers scored victories in the policy debates and the word "socialism" was flourished with uninhibited abandon. On the key issue of leadership, the strength of the moderates was apparent. Romanow retained a narrow lead for two ballots until Mitchell's retirement released a hundred ballots to elect Blakeney. Close to another hundred refused to vote. Hard-core Wafflers, they insisted that there really was no choice.

In Ontario, the leadership question had apparently been settled in 1968 when Donald MacDonald had decisively beaten James Renwick. However, by early 1970, it was obvious that Stephen Lewis, a former Renwick backer, was manoeuvring for a challenge of his own, building alliances within the provincial caucus and serving as party labour critic in an attempt to win union support. For MacDonald, it was a bitter discovery. His own prestige in the province at large was rising, confirmed by a by-election victory in Middlesex South in the autumn of 1969. A second leadership challenge would be fatal blow to his own standing and to party unity. After attempts by senior

labour leaders and the Ontario party executive to dis-
courage Lewis had failed, MacDonald weighed the consequences for his party against his own long years of
struggle and calmly announced his intention to resign.

Until the end of July, Lewis was the uncontested
heir-apparent. Senior union leaders had discovered, somewhat to their chagrin, that he had quietly lined up many
of the second-level leaders in their organizations as well as
Dennis MacDermott, the aggressive new leader of the
United Autoworkers in Canada. Accepting MacDonald's
obvious hint that a uncontested succession would do the
least harm to the party, most of the senior union officials
joined the Lewis camp. Only a few remained to give
private support when Walter Pitman, the former New Party
M.P. and currently the provincial member for Peterborough, was persuaded to enter the contest. For some of
his backers, he was a rallying point in their bitterness at
the treatment of MacDonald; for many he seemed a more
likely figure to attract Ontario voters. According to
Professor John Wilson, a supporter, Pitman was "the
personification both of progressive change and of cautious
common sense" which Ontarians wanted in a political
leader. The Lewis campaign, headed by Gerald Caplan,
answered that Ontarians really wanted a radical alternative
for their discontents. Whatever the provinces's electorate
felt, Lewis plainly reflected the wishes of a large, ebullient
convention by a margin of 1,188 votes to 642.

Though the Waffle had run a leadership candidate in
Saskatchewan, the more sophisticated Ontario branch
chose different tactics. A pre-convention Waffle meeting
heard both candidates, proclaimed that neither was a
"socialist," and proceeded to concentrate on achieving
policy victories and winning control of the party executive. As the badly divided party leadership threw itself
into the Lewis-Pitman race, Waffle spokesmen dominated

the convention microphones and committees, delighting delegates with roundhouse assaults on American corporations, resource barons and "right-wingers" in the party leadership. By the time the moderates realized what was happening, the convention had endorsed Waffle-inspired resolutions calling, among other things, for nationalization of energy resource industries and abortion on demand. Delegates were even within an ace of adopting an Ontario version of the Waffle manifesto as a statement of party goals. A last-minute salvage operation reversed the tide but could not undo some of the Waffle triumphs.

From the moderate standpoint, forcing a contest had probably been a mistake. The chances of beating Lewis, even for a contender as respected as Pitman, were slim. Campaigning as "Pitman for Premier," the challenger and his team used their opportunity for public attention to speak to Ontario voters while Lewis concentrated on the short-range need to arouse the emotions of party members. Not only did the contest allow the Waffle considerable freedom to control the convention, it presented Lewis, the quintessential "party" man, as the rhetorician of a socialist "movement." Far from moderating his public image as some Pitman supporters had hoped, Lewis played to the version of the Ontario electorate his advisers had concocted for him.

While Lewis and Blakeney prepared to test their appeal with a wider public than NDP convention delegates, there were faint signs of life from the Atlantic provinces where the party, like the CCF, had so far achieved little more than a holding operation. In the autumn of 1969, an erratic and not notably temperate member of the New Brunswick legislature had abandoned the Liberal government to sit as a New Democrat. There was no great regret when he returned to his own party in the spring. In Newfoundland, the NDP had made virtually no headway since the disintegration of Ed Finn's Newfoundland Democratic Party. From a tiny bridgehead at Memorial University, the party reached unavailingly to find some new indigenous roots. Negotiations with Tom Burgess, future leader of the New Labrador Party, foundered on his desire to have a paid position on the Steelworkers' staff. Approaches to Richard Cashin, a former Liberal M.P., were momentarily more promising but he turned his energies to the more immediate task of organizing fishermen.

Only in Nova Scotia was there discernible progress. Throughout the Sixties, the NDP had consisted of a small but valiant outpost of supporters in Halifax and a slightly larger but ageing group on Cape Breton Island, reproducing in miniature most of the strains and jealousies which traditionally divide the island and the mainland. The leader, Professor James Aitchison, was a respected and selfless worker for the party, with little prospect or expectation of leading it to a position of influence or power. In 1969, the dominance of the Halifax group was challenged by two abrasive young men, Jeremy Akerman, a former radio announcer, and Paul MacEwan, a teacher, who set themsleves the task of organizing for victory in Cape Breton. Amidst general scepticism and with what meagre finances the federal party could spare and their own supporters could collect, Akerman and MacEwan were rewarded for their labours by election to the Nova Scotia legislature on October 13th, 1970.

In 1971, elections were due in Saskatchewan, Alberta and Ontario. Camp's law of political longevity may allow a provincial government a good second chance but it does not promise a third. By May 25th, 1971, when Ross Thatcher declared an election on June 23rd, his confidence in success had to depend more on his opponents' weakness than his own strength. If there was any group Thatcher had not alienated, complained his lieutenant, Dave Steuart,

it was because the premier had not yet met it. In fact, the Liberal leader campaigned as though he was trying to topple a government, not retain it, flailing the NDP and the Trudeau regime with equal vehemence, demanding labour courts as a weapon against the province's tiny labour movement, and promising a second pulp mill for the province at a time when the NDP was getting growing support for its opposition to fast sale of Saskatchewan resources.

While Thatcher flew over the province in a chartered airplane, Blakeney rode from hamlet to farmyard in a chartered bus, focussing on nagging issues like the Thatcher government's deterrent fees for Medicare users or a ruthlessly gerrymandered election map. When the Liberal slogan boasted "They can do more for Saskatchewan," Blakeney suggested that perhaps they had done enough already, with low farm prices, unemployment and inflation. Instead, re-defining its initials as "New Deal for People," the NDP stressed land bank and credit legislation to save the family farm, reduction in property taxes, help for small businesses and a determination to get a better return from the province's oil and mining industries. The Liberal appeal for "growth" was answered by an NDP emphasis on "quality of life." Thatcher, who had begun the campaigning by patronising Blakeney as "little Allan," woke up to his danger with a last-minute refrain of a familiar campaign song, "socialism versus free enterprise." It was too late. On June 23rd, Saskatchewan voters gave the NDP 55.2 per cent of their support and forty-five seats in the most one-sided victory for the Canadian Left since the 1940s. A shattered, demoralized Liberal party could not even muster the courtesy to thank its defeated premier; it was the NDP rally in Regina which turned from its celebration to cheer Ross Thatcher as a worthy opponent. Less than a month later, he was dead.

◁ Allan Blakeney. Saskatchewan's return to a left-wing government in 1971 demonstrated that the farmer-labour alliance was politically possible. Blakeney, himself, was a former federal NDP president and a CCF cabinet minister. (Saskatchewan NDP)

Blakeney took office with the smoothness and assurance of experience. A cabinet drawn from the moderate majority (only one had endorsed the Waffle manifesto) started to turn the province around. Contracts for the controversial pulp mill and a Liberal-sponsored iron mine were cancelled for re-negotiation, a Family Farm Protection Act relieved small farmers of impossible debt burdens, Thatcher's anti-union legislation was repealed, deterrent fees for visits to doctors and hospitals were cancelled and all fees for patients over sixty-five were abolished. There was more to come as the new government went on to tackle more complex problems like its land bank proposals and the foreign ownership of the province's farm land.

Just as the Manitoba victory had influenced the British Columbia election in 1969, the second NDP electoral success fuelled the already surging expectations of the Ontario party. At the end of 1970, the dull grey John Robarts announced his forthcoming retirement. His heir would be William Davis, the Minister of Education who had floated almost unscathed by criticism through the buoyant Sixties. However, at the convention, the certainty faded. Allan Lawrence, a mildly maverick cabinet minister with backing from rich Torontonians and the party's middle class youth, chased Davis through five ballots before allowing him the prize. To an outsider, the Tories appeared deeply divided, with a leader who barely commanded the support of half his party.

Ontario Tories would not have lasted in office since 1943 without a powerful sense of survival. Davis co-opted the Lawrence organizers to his own team. He also turned to his American political kinfolk, employing Market Opinion Research, a Detroit firm which had worked for the Republicans, to programme his campaign. MOR gave Davis his strategy. A survey showed that Ontario voters liked Davis but considered his NDP opponent "the least competent, the least trustworthy and the least sociable of the three party leaders." Unemployment was the chief issue; economic nationalism issues were only mentioned by 8.8 per cent of those polled. On a subsidiary but troublesome issue, MOR found that a big majority of voters opposed giving more money to Catholic schools, a policy favoured by Liberals and New Democrats. Shortly before the writs were issued, proclaiming that it should not become an election issue, Davis announced his own stand: no money. His support among middle-class Torontonians also jumped when he stopped the city's controversial Spadina Expressway. Both acts boosted the premier's "decisiveness" quotient; both were pre-planned to be popular. By September, when the campaign officially began, the Conservatives had built themselves into enviable strength.

Even Liberals wrote off their own party as a threat in the 1971 elections and conceded that the main opposition would come from the NDP. Davis had helped give that impression in the spring when he ran his own "socialism versus free enterprise" campaign to load up the Conservative campaign coffers for a special effort. The NDP itself felt more confident than usual. It was well prepared, well organized and, by its own modest standards, well financed. Province-wide expenditures eventually totalled $197,000 (half from constituency association quotas, a quarter from unions, the rest from fund-raising efforts like the sale of campaign buttons). At least $300,000 was spent by local campaigns. More than fourteen organizers had worked for a year to develop canvassing organizations and more were available from sympathetic unions and other provincial sections of the party as soon as the campaign started.

There was only one major economy. Unlike their

opponents, the NDP had no survey to guide the campaign or the intuition of Lewis and his advisers. Instead, working on their own conception of Davis, the issues and the electorate, the NDP campaign committee offered Lewis as "a fully accredited moderate," stressed the party's forthright enthusiasm for economic independence and avoided the monotonous reiteration of basic issues like taxes and housing which had been a feature of MacDonald's 1967 campaign. Instead, more exciting items from the party platform were featured: a guaranteed annual income, free tuition, salaries for housewives, the extension of medicare to cover drugs and dental treatment. To help display its new leader, the party supplemented the usual campaign bus with an elderly airplane chartered for long northern hauls.

If the Conservative party's surveys were accurate, the NDP could hardly have done better if the Tories themselves had given the orders. As for their own campaign, the Conservatives emphasized job creation and a sense of economic purpose ideally suited to match the sudden chill after the proclamation of American economic countermeasures in August, 1971. While the NDP leader challenged Ontario voters, the Conservatives, with their anodyne "Call me Bill" image of the premier, sought to reassure them. The result, on October 21st, was derived from the highest turn-out of the provincial voters since 1898. The Davis campaign netted 44.5 per cent of the vote and seventy-eight seats; the Liberals won 27.8 per cent of the vote and twenty seats and the NDP stayed almost where it had been in 1967, with 27.2 per cent and nineteen seats.

For Lewis, it was a bitter evening after a year and a half of virtually non-stop campaigning. As newspapers boasted of a Tory landslide, he discovered that he had barely held his own seat. There were five NDP victories over incumbent Liberals or Conservatives but seven other sitting members, among them Walter Pitman, had been beaten. The party had even been narrowly edged out of its minimum goal of replacing the Liberals as official opposition. The Liberals had fallen, but not far enough. There were NDP gains in the north and in normally barren eastern Ontario but in industrial cities like Hamilton, Oshawa and in the outskirts of Toronto, Conservative talk of jobs and security obviously meant more than the challenge of economic nationalism. Once again, the NDP had failed to connect with masses of potential working-class supporters. For a leader who had staked so much on his own capacity to articulate a political mood and to sense the barometer of public feeling, it was a double disillusionment.

Not all provincial governments held the secret of eternal life. On August 31st, 1971, Peter Lougheed and the Conservatives ended the thirty-five year regime of Alberta's Social Credit League. Alberta New Democrats, long hardened to disappointment, could take comfort in the election of their provincial leader, Grant Notley, in a Peace River constituency.

VII. Clarification

The newspapers which recorded the outcome of the Ontario NDP leadership convention reported the kidnapping of James Cross. In the ensuing days, Canadians watched in dismay as events they had associated with remote Latin American dictatorships took place in their own country. Political terrorism, blackmail, a revolting murder, mass arrests, troops with steel helmets and machine guns, the startling activation of the half-forgotten War Measures Act: here, with a vengeance, was that "smack of firm government" Trudeau had represented for Canadian voters in 1968.

In retrospect, it became easy to say that the government had raised an enormous hammer against a handful of unbalanced fanatics, acting out the revolutionary fantasies of the nationalist elite. The extraordinary proposal for a special government to take over Quebec, associated with Claude Ryan, was nothing more than another manifestation of the self-importance of that same Montreal elite. As for the evident psychological collapse of the Bourassa government or the need to shock would-be revolutionaries from dreams back into reality, these were reasons for the War Measures Act which the Trudeau government could hardly be expected to articulate in

◁ David Lewis during the 1972 election campaign. With the brilliantly orchestrated denunciation of the "Corporate Welfare Bums," thousands of party members who had forgotten why they belonged suddenly remembered. (Information Canada)

public. In the absence of such an explanation (or perhaps even if it had been offered), sixteen members of the New Democratic Party caucus rose alone in the midst of the clamor to oppose the federal government's action.

At a time when a tired prime minister spoke of "bleeding hearts," when Robert Stanfield, whatever his private reservations, stood with the majority, when Réal Caouette demanded that the revolutionaries be shot by firing squad, it was an act of collective courage. Coast to coast, most powerfully in Quebec itself, Canadians backed the government and vilified the NDP as an alliance of cowards, traitors and secret separatists. To an impressive degree, the party membership stood firm. It understood the position of those who had sided with the government; it admired the sixteen who had not. Some were reminded that, in 1942, the CCF had also been vilified for its protests when Japanese Canadians had been subjected to mass deportation under the same War Measures Act. It was one of the stands that had added distinction to the CCF's record. By November, when the party accepted the principle of the Public Order (Temporary Measures) Act as the price imposed by the government for withdrawing the War Measures Act, the civil libertarians had been aroused and even turned on the NDP for its apparent surrender. The public mood changed more slowly. A December Gallup poll showed the Liberals at an almost unprecedented fifty-nine per cent and the NDP slumped from twenty to twelve per cent. By the spring, though, the party had recovered and, in a by-election in the Ontario constituency of Brant on May 31st, 1971, captured a traditionally strong Liberal seat. There is nothing so mutable in politics as the public's memory.

Paradoxically, the party's position in the October crisis damaged it nowhere so much as in Quebec. Since 1968, the NDP's affairs in the province had deteriorated sadly. Ill

and exhausted, Robert Cliche could no longer afford to
carry on as leader. His successor, Roland Morin, an
interpreter and former union official, persuaded a reluctant party to contest the 1970 provincial election. The
result was a humiliating disaster. Between them, the
party's thirteen candidates collected a derisory 4,130 votes
– 0.15 per cent of the total. The strong separatist showing
in the 1970 election and the ensuing October crisis ended a
bitter dilemma for many of the faithful CCF and NDP
supporters. Despite NDP efforts to appeal to French
Canadians, it had remained dependent on English-speaking
Montrealers for most of its money, members and energy.
The rise of the Parti Québecois meant, for many of them,
that the NDP was a luxury they could no longer afford.
The party's pathetic showing in the April election indicated the disaffection. The October crisis confirmed it:
even the veteran CCFer, Frank Scott, reluctantly agreed
with the Trudeau government's response. So, too, did
Michael Oliver, the NDP's first president.

When the remnants of the NDP gathered in a church
basement in Montreal on February 19th-21st, 1971, it had
become a very different organization. Most of the leading
figures of the previous eight years were gone. Robert
Cliche appeared, almost out of loyalty, to lend a symbolic
presence but a new leader and a changed mood were
symptoms of change. Raymond Laliberté, the latest
Quebec president, had impressive credentials as the former
head of Quebec's militant teacher's union, the C.E.Q. A
thin, intense intellectual with a wispy beard and a grating
voice, he was a self-persuaded socialist, immune from most
of the pragmatic gradualism of those who had grown with
the faith. His chief lieutenant, Emile Boudreau, a Steelworkers official in Montreal, held an executive position in
the Parti Québecois. In an attempt to appeal to those who
might be attracted to the NDP by its stand in October,

convention organizers had proclaimed an "open" meeting: anyone who came could vote. The resulting influx facilitated the transformation; it probably did not change it. It was an invitation to those who had felt themselves "radicalized" by the October events, to those who had hitherto felt themselves too radical for the NDP and to those who now felt that the NDP might be able to carry the twenty-three per cent separatist vote in federal elections.

Less than two hundred delegates and hangers-on went to the week-end meeting but they transformed the NDP in Quebec. When they emerged, a coalition of quasi-separatists had taken over the party, forged an alliance with the Waffle group and presented, virtually as an ultimatum, what should be the NDP's next policy on federalism. The "Canadian party," as the federal NDP was now called, must recognize the unfettered right of Quebec to self-determination. The phrase was not new. It was hallowed in innumerable United Nations resolutions, approved by Claude Ryan and *Le Devoir* and endorsed, long since, by the Waffle. Its meaning, robbed of the exquisite rhetoric which soon embellished it, was that Quebec would have the unilateral right to decide whatever she liked inside or outside Confederation. To illustrate the theory by practice, the Quebec party proclaimed that it was entitled to its own constitution, that it would offer its own programme and that the "Canadian party" could conform or not as it pleased.

The church basement convention got national publicity. Waffle spokesmen proclaimed a major triumph and the news media echoed the claim. Inevitably, the reports and the claim ignored some of the complicated details. The NDP had not, for example, actually been captured by the Parti Québecois itself. Laliberté was not precisely a separatist; he was prepared to accept a loose, almost diaphanous, federalism. His chief feeling was that the entire national issue had to be cleared from the agenda of Quebec politics before socialism could be seriously considered. Others, even Boudreau, had become somewhat disillusioned by the P.Q. — not for its nationalism, of course, but because it was insufficiently radical. For the NDP across Canada, as for the press and the public, these were nuances which hardly made much difference. The notion that "self-determination," once obtained, might never be exercised, was urged by Waffle leaders and by Laliberté himself. All that meant, surely, was that Quebec would have a weapon to obtain the best of both federalism and independence. Across Canada, the party would be condemned for making a treasonable deal with Quebec separatists in the hope of a handful of extra seats in parliament.

In retrospect, the NDP might simply have disavowed its troublesome Quebec section. A year later, it would do precisely that with its vestigial New Brunswick section when it briefly fell into the hands of a coterie of Fredericton revolutionaries. What was the Quebec NDP, after all, but a few hundred paid-up members and an annual subsidy of $15,000? In the winter of 1971, such forcefulness was inconceivable. On the eve of a possible federal election, it would expose the party's claim to a Quebec wing as the Potemkin village it really was. It would have endangered the chances of running a few score of token candidates in French Canada on which the NDP's claim to national party status depended. It would have provoked an open battle with the Waffle for which neither the party nor its leaders were prepared. Above all, it would have demanded tough, concerted leadership at a time when it was not available. Allan Blakeney, the party president, was immersed in preparations for his forthcoming Saskatchewan election, while T. C. Douglas had seen his role, quite properly, as virtually a caretaker leader since his return to Parliament in 1969; if his successor chose to deal with the Waffle or Quebec, he would at least find them in the party. Ever since Douglas had announced in October, 1969, that he was definitely stepping down, the federal party secretary, Clifford Scotton, had been fully engaged in preparing for the Ottawa leadership convention. It was an undertaking comparable in scope and complexity to the original New Party Founding Convention.

By the winter of 1971, the NDP's leadership race had acquired all five of its contestants. To ensure fairness, the party drew up elaborate rules and illustrated its own principles of campaign finance by allowing each candidate a thousand dollar grant and limiting him to a maximum expenditure of $10,500. To help further, the five were shepherded through a schedule of all-candidate meetings across the country. Ed Broadbent had been the first to declare, basing his claims on his credentials as an academic radical, his success in getting elected and his links with a number of trade unionists. John Harney, the bilingual former Ontario secretary, had worked publicly at Winnipeg and quietly thereafter to extend his support, particularly among consituency moderates who saw Lewis as too old, Broadbent as too woolly and Laxer, the Waffle candidate, as political suicide. James Laxer had been fielded only after much Waffle strategical pondering: cool, articulate and disarming, he was undoubtedly their most attractive personality. Frank Howard, a veteran loner in the caucus since his election in 1957, was the only candidate who did not come from Ontario. All four were overshadowed by David Lewis, the Polish immigrant boy who had risen from Montreal's Jewish ghetto through a Rhodes Scholarship and his own brilliance and toughness to become the undoubted guiding force of the CCF and the NDP since the 1940s. No one could doubt his qualifications or his claims to the party leadership; some could wonder about his age, his flexibility and his strength. Far more serious as an obstacle were the bitter, remorseless enemies he had acquired in thirty-five years of fighting to impose his own concept of social democracy on the party. Lewis might be the ablest, the most clear-minded, the most forceful leader the CCF or the NDP had produced; he was not the best-loved.

Lewis's chief antagonist at the 1971 convention would be the Waffle group. Encouraged by success in polarizing debate within the party and by the realization that the party leadership was on the defensive, the group organized vigorously. Its prime target was the weaker constituencies and those where, perhaps, barely a tenth of the membership appeared for a general meeting. Concentrating its strength, caucusing in advance, it was not difficult to dominate the delegate elections or to win approval for Waffle resolutions. If regular members were not prepared to sit through interminable debates, procedural wrangling and florid rhetoric, that was their problem. It rapidly became the concern of a group of moderates, based on the party's federal council, who decided that in the Ottawa convention the Waffle would not win by default. An array of draft resolutions, matching the Waffle formulations, was presented through sympathetic constituencies and affiliated organizations, plans were laid to provide speakers before and at the convention and limited efforts were made to ensure that sympathetic delegates were elected, all independent of the leadership campaigns. To show its flag, the group presented its philosophy in a booklet entitled *NDP NOW*. Launched only a few months before the convention, the NDP Now group, like the Waffle in 1969, was no more than a cadre of like-minded people in search of wider support.

It found it, initially, in a sharp, pre-convention battle

for control of the resolutions committee, the funnel
through which material was transmitted to delegates for
their decisions. When the smoke cleared, the Waffle had
won only a quarter of the positions on the committee and
convention resolutions were accordingly bereft, as a
Montreal reporter commented, of "the rhetorical symbols
– words like imperialism, exploitation or even socialism –
which turn on the Wafflers and, probably, turn off the
voters." Control of the drafting of resolutions by moderates meant that the Waffle was compelled to rally support
to "refer back" statements for the incorporation of its
own ideas and verbal symbols. That gave Waffle spokesmen
the advantage of the offensive but it provided the NDP
Now organizers with a simple signal system – all references
back were to be defeated. Apart from some symbolic
victories – banning candidates' signs and placards from the
convention floor, changing the timetable for a demonstration – the Waffle, for the first time, encountered an
impermeable wall of opposition to its policies.

The Quebec resolution could not be disposed of so
simply. For the first time, delegates were not prepared to
give a blank cheque to upholders of the latest nationalist
slogan. Experience with "special status" in 1968 had not
been forgotten. The open alliance with the Waffle cost
Laliberté and his group the previous automatic sympathy
of party leaders. Still, the urge to find a compromise
remained almost desperate. A major leadership convention,
with extensive national coverage, was hardly the moment
to unveil the disintegration of NDP support in French
Canada. After anguished sessions, the resolutions committee grudgingly accepted a laborious statement which
acknowledged that if "one of our provinces were to choose
to separate freely and democratically, it would be madness
to attempt to restrain it by force." With Waffle encourage-
ment, the new Quebec leadership rejected the compromise

out of hand. Briefly, the majority view hardened and a fresh version of the statement appeared, implicitly rejecting the earlier formulas of "two nations" and "special status" and asserting: "There is no question of the right of Canadians to question Confederation. Nor is there any doubt that the existence of our country depends on the free consent of all our people. The unity of our country cannot be based on force. However, the business of the NDP is to work for a united Canada, on a basis which will do full justice to all our people." After checking to see that Mr. Trudeau had made an identical observation, the drafters further conceded that Canada could not be held together by force.

Compromise resumed as more moderate leadership candidates were consulted and tacit approval was obtained from those Quebec members who might be needed to put together a new party if the Laliberté group bolted. That meant a further, lengthy statement promising that the federal and Quebec parties would continue, after the convention, to try to resolve their differences. The final version was taken before the full convention, exposed to the kind of full-dress, televised debate which the Waffle and "United Canada" resolutions had received at Winnipeg, and adopted 853 to 423. Having won its policy victories, the NDP Now group publicly announced its dissolution.

In contrast to Liberal and Conservative conventions, the leadership race was virtually sandwiched between policy sessions. Nomination speeches, a final debate and occasional interventions in policy debates had helped Laxer and Harney and probably Howard, confirmed Lewis in his traditional role as a convention "heavy" and fatally damaged Broadbent's chances. When balloting began on the afternoon of April 24th, the ranking was predictable; the relative strengths were not. At 661 votes, Lewis's support showed the absence of a hundred or more trade union delegates whose promised presence might have given him a badly-needed first ballot victory. Laxer, with 378, was second; Harney had 299, Broadbent 236 and Howard had 124, more than predicted but too few to stay in the contest. Surprise came with the second ballot. Instead of a rush to Lewis to end the race, the four remaining candidates kept their places, with Harney gaining proportionately and Broadbent falling: the results were Lewis, 715; Laxer, 407; Harney, 347 and Broadbent 223. On the third ballot, a natural switch between middle-of-the road candidates could have put Harney in second place and perhaps won him the contest. Instead, a hundred Broadbent people went to Laxer, driven by a surprising bitterness between the two closest camps. The results were Lewis, 742; Laxer, 508; Harney, 431. A fourth ballot ended it as two generations of Lewis enemies moved out to grab yellow Laxer badges, the leading Harney supporters headed for Lewis and their candidate sat grimly alone with his shattered ambition. The final count was 1046 for Lewis, 612 for Laxer, a shabby triumph for a veteran who deserved better from his party. As Laxer supporters pounded their feet and shouted "Power to the People" in the approved American style, their candidate headed for the podium to make the graceful gesture of declaring the vote unanimous.

When the convention dissolved, two critical pieces of unfinished business remained: the Waffle and Quebec. Neither problem had been much improved by the unexpectedly prolonged leadership contest.

On the Quebec NDP, Lewis faced the choices the party had avoided in February: he could ignore the Laliberté group and try to patch together the earlier Quebec NDP or he could seek to negotiate. He chose the latter course, armed with the implied blank cheque in the second half of the convention resolution. He found Laliberté and Boudreau in a more accommodating frame of mind. The former had decided that a promise not to support civil war was not so far from self-determination after all and, in any case, his group's claim to policy autonomy had not yet been challenged. Boudreau, for his part, had tried the political water in a by-election in Chambly on May 31st and discovered that the riding's separatists would not, after all, support the NDP. After six laborious meetings, much drafting, and toing and froing between Montreal and Ottawa, a brand new policy and the latest slogan, "*une constituante*," had emerged. To resolve the problems of Canada, the NDP would call a grand constitutional conference at which all Canadians would be represented — governments, oppositions, provinces, cities, even the native people "in a manner determined by themselves." Like many political compromises, the new formula was absurd and naive. It ignored the problems which a large and disparate assembly would face in arriving at agreement in a public forum. It ignored the problems of ratification. It ignored the problems of content. Instead, it patched over a problem, restored the illusion that the party was a factor in French Canada and preserved what a Quebec NDP spokesman, sociologist Gabriel Gagnon, admitted to be a pre-election truce.

The Waffle problem could not be resolved by words. Two years of conciliation, accommodation and hope had broken down on the eve of the 1971 convention. For the Waffle, four days of non-stop policy setbacks were forgotten after Laxer's unexpectedly powerful showing. News coverage of the convention emphasized the polarization of the party and suggested that Lewis would have to conciliate his left wing to bring the NDP back together. Promptly, he made it clear that he would do no such thing. Convention delegates elected only a single Waffler to the party's new executive. With the former Ontario leader, Donald MacDonald, as the NDP's new president, Lewis could count on firm executive support.

For two years, party battles would be essentially provincial. Before the 1971 Saskatchewan election, Waffle leader Don Mitchell announced that the party would get no help from the group unless it pronounced its more radical policies with the requisite firmness. Blakeney ignored the ultimatum. In Ontario, Stephen Lewis was not so nonchalant. On Feburary 21st, 1971, he launched his first public attack on the group and its public utterances. A month later, the Waffle's Ontario chairman, Stephen Penner, riposted with a well-publicised attack on the party's official programme, terming it dishonest and complaining that the word "socialist" appeared only once in its seventy-three pages. As the provincial elections approached, some Wafflers went after key nominations. Penner captured the candidacy in the downtown Toronto riding of Dovercourt; Bruce Kidd, a well-known athlete and Waffler, defeated the party's research director, Marion Bryden, in a contest for the party-held seat of Beaches. In the autumn election, Wafflers fought almost autonomous campaigns, collecting sympathisers from other consti- tuencies to work in favoured areas at the expense of other candidates and to the particular benefit of Penner. Other Wafflers made sure that Stephen Lewis, at public meetings, was regularly questioned about more controversial features of the NDP program such as nationalization of resource industries and abortion on demand.

In the dreary aftermath of the Ontario campaign, Stephen Lewis had plenty of opportunity to recall the Waffle contribution — and the embarrassing fact that Penner had only been narrowly defeated in Dovercourt. Waffle activities were no longer limited to conferences, meetings and internal party agitation. Increasingly, the group marched into labour battles under its own flag, grabbing headlines and attempting to impose its own strategies. There was a growing affinity between Waffle leaders and J. Kent Rowley, an inveterate left-wing foe of the mainstream Canadian labour movement who had suddenly become a darling of the nationalists through his raids on international unions. After the 1971 election, the Waffle voice in the Ontario NDP grew stronger. Election-oriented members and supporters resumed their normal lives, leaving the usual small band of militants and faithful to carry on the chores of a political party between campaigns. Waffle activity, for both newcomers and jaded veterans, was an appealing alternative to collecting memberships, selling dance tickets, organizing raffles and the other indispensable drudgery of a self-financed political organization.

Lewis's own work of rebuilding and maintaining the party ran into road-blocks. At a party meeting in St. Catherines, Wafflers jeered and heckled him, virtually driving him from the platform. A Waffle conference in Windsor in January, 1972, designed to extend the group's trade union following, provided a platform for labour malcontents of every political persuasion. Press reports revelled in denunciations of international unions and their leaders. For the party's key labour supporters, the Windsor meeting was a catalyst for growing misgivings about Waffle activity. Indoctrinated in the political stereotypes of the American union scene, few political commentators seemed aware that most Ontario labour leaders had even deeper roots in socialism than in unionism. Men and women like David Archer, president of the Ontario Federation of Labour, Iona Samis, secretary of the Canadian Food and Allied Workers or Lynn Williams, the cool, articulate former graduate student who was soon to take over District 6 of the Steelworkers, had spent their youth in the CCF or its radical youth movement. Almost consciously, they had turned to the labour movement rather than to politics in the late Forties and Fifties because they saw it as the only framework for the mass base on which democratic socialism could be built. Others, with roots in the British Labour Party, shared their goals. Increasingly, they perceived the Waffle as a threat to their strategy. After two years of reluctance to get involved, the party's trade union leaders saw the January meeting in Windsor as a challenge. If Lewis was prepared to fight, they would see the battle through to a finish.

A constituency resolution addressed to the Ontario NDP council meeting in Oshawa on March 18th, 1972, condemning the Waffle, provided the opportunity. With both sides warned, attendance was heavy at the drab union hall but few were braced for Stephen Lewis's forceful and uncompromising attack. The Waffle, he proclaimed, had poisoned the atmosphere of debate within the party, had maintained the separate structure of a party within a party and had displayed a "sneering, contemptuous attitude towards official trade unionism and the labour leadership." Much of his ammunition was drawn from reports of a secret Waffle meeting in Hamilton only a few weeks before. A long and bitter debate ended only when the party secretary, Gordon Brigden, moved that the problem be referred to the Ontario NDP executive for a report. A vote of 157 to 62 suggested the relative strength of the forces.

For the next three months, the Ontario party was in turmoil. A three member committee, headed by the provincial president, Gordon Vichert, and including the party treasurer, John Brewin and the former Waffler, Gerald Caplan, toured the province to hear opinions. The Waffle, by no means meekly submissive, crowded the committee meetings, shouted down opposing voices and flatly rejected Lewis's criticisms. The group's 8,000 word brief uncompromisingly asserted the Waffle's right to exist, denounced the party leadership and implied that the real villain was, of course, the trade union leadership. If polarization had been intended by both Lewis and the Waffle, it happened. A neutral, even mildly sympathetic committee returned traumatised by the vitriolic mood it had encountered. Instead of the expected compromise, the ensuing report announced that the issue was no longer about democratic debate or whether the party should be radicalized; it had become a question of whether the majority in the NDP could tolerate a ceaseless assault on its principles, policies, structures and leadership. "Our party exists to fulfil certain purposes which have been decided upon by a majority of its members. In our judgement, the fulfilment of those purposes takes precedence over any absolute rights of unfettered freedom, and when the assertion of such rights threatens to undermine the Party's overriding function, the party is entitled, even obligated, to assert its rights." The committee proposed a membership-controlled study of party operations, communications, even the trade union relationship, but it concluded, unequivocally, that the NDP could no longer afford organized, structured opposition groups. The Waffle would have to dissolve.

The report, issued on May 6th, only added to the clamor of the struggle. Urged on, perhaps a little hypocritically, by the newspapers, individuals and groups thrust themselves forward in the role of peacemaker. Two former federal leadership aspirants renewed their rivalry as spokesmen for different plans. John Harney proposed that the Waffle become an affiliated organization, forcing it to reveal its strength but liberating it for its own activities. It was an ingenious scheme which, however, found favour with neither side. More common were proposals for codes of conduct to help guide groups and individuals within the party. It was Ed Broadbent who helped to steer through the so-called Riverdale motion which formed the basis for the eventual party decision. Its principle was simple: the rights of groups to caucus and organize to change party policies and leader had to be recognized. In the angry mood of the party, that would only be possible if the name Waffle disappeared. For the Wafflers, compromise had not seemed necessary or appropriate. Insistent claims that they were being "purged" encouraged press and party members alike to cast them in the congenial role of martyr. Only in the final weeks, at last realizing that they had painted themselves into a corner, did Waffle leaders even consider concessions. Party leaders and the executive moved first, persuaded that the Riverdale motion reflected a basic uneasiness in the riding associations. The Waffle, which by now faced only a reprimand and loss of its name, refused. Instead, it came to Orillia on June 23rd more intransigent than ever.

The meeting next day in the sleepy little Ontario city climaxed three of the most searing months in the Ontario party's history. For five hours, the compromise resolution was denounced as "the War Measures Act" of the NDP and defended as the minimum condition for restoring civilized relations within the party. "I, too, am a socialist who wished to fight for a free Canada," Stephen Lewis hurled at his critics, "but I want to fight without the Waffle forever an encumbrance around my neck." By a vote of 217 to 88, he had his wish.

For almost two months, the Waffle kept the Ontario party waiting for its reaction to the demand for dissolution. Two Toronto riding associations announced that they were on strike, refusing to pay their debts to the provincial organization. The Quebec NDP, momentarily forgetting its insistence on provincial autonomy, condemned the Ontario section and, in Saskatchewan, the Waffle an-

nounced that it would do nothing until the Ontario NDP
rescinded its decision. Four constituencies which had
nominated prominent Wafflers for the forthcoming federal
election waited with rising impatience until mid-July when
all four announced that they would not run. A month
later, on August 19th-20th, the group held its last meeting
as part of the NDP. By then, it had already split. With an
election approaching, many of its fringe supporters had
glumly accepted the Orillia decision. Others, led by
Stephen Penner, announced that they would cling to the
party to disrupt it in every way possible. A few of them
were arbitrarily excluded when the meeting opened in a
hall in Delaware, a small town outside London. A majority
of those who attended agreed to follow Laxer and Watkins
out of the party and into a "Movement for an Independent
Socialist Canada." The initials of the new organization,
MISC, did little to encourage even sympathisers to take it
very seriously.

   Like most great political dramas, the Waffle affair ended
in anti-climax. It was a misfortune for both the NDP and
the leading Wafflers but it was probably inevitable. If the
group had dissolved in 1969, as the NDP Now group did at
the end of the 1971 convention, both its influence and its
potential would have remained. By persisting, its leaders,
despite their media reputation as political tacticians, were
to qualify as losers. After three years, according to their
own insistent judgement, they left the NDP even more
"reactionary" than they had found it. The leading Wafflers
had begun with positions of prestige and influence in the
party; systematically, they had lost them. The transformation of a powerful pressure group, mobilizing a third
of the voting strength of a national political party, into a
sectarian study club, meeting in closed session to avoid
capture by Trotskyites, must count among the more
dramatic reversals of fortune in recent Canadian political

James Laxer. More than any other Waffle leader, he earned the respect of NDP leaders and affection from party members. Trapped by the ideology of the students' movement, his influence was lost. (Ontario NDP)   ▷

Whether or not Stephen and David Lewis wanted the Waffle out of the NDP, Watkins and Laxer had manoeuvred themselves into a position which meant that one side or the other had to go. (Aislin) ▽

history. The NDP, too, had suffered. It could not afford a hemorrhage of young and vigorous supporters, or the bitterness of many veteran members who could not easily understand why decisive action had been necessary. Despite the obvious decision by the Waffle supporters to remove themselves from the party, it was easier to believe the claims of Wafflers and news media alike that the party establishment had purged its liveliest critics.

The problem for the NDP was due to its own ambivalence. It was and behaved like a mass party of the democratic Left; it also presented itself as a socialist movement. Those who abandoned traditional allegiances, plucked up their skirts and crossed the Rubicon to true socialism would inevitably find the Waffle more attractive than the messy, compromising New Democratic Party, with its pedestrian concern for fund-raising, canvassing and picking up members. Politics could become a religion, in which even the solemn incantation of the word "socialism" would become mystically satisfying. To the majority in the party, routinely loyal to what was natural, logical and sensible, such a millenarian enthusiasm might seem marvellous and enviable but also a little foreign and suspect. In its lengthy brief to the Ontario party, the Waffle had suggested that solid commitment (among trade union affiliates, for example) was more important than mere endorsement. It was a persuasive argument if the NDP had been basically a dedicated but doctrinaire socialist movement. Eleven years of history and a Canadian political culture had already made it something else: it was, structurally, and ideologically, if not yet numerically, a mass party.

For David Lewis, the Ontario preoccupation with the Waffle had been infuriating. An election was certain in 1972; if it had come in the spring, it would have found almost a third of his party deep in fratricidal struggle. In

February, the country had smiled when the New Brunswick NDP had been captured by a tiny clique which
travelled even to the left of the Waffle. An embarrassing
month ensued before control was recaptured by more
responsible leaders. Throughout the Ontario battle, the
elder Lewis, refuting his stereotype, urged moderate
compromise. And only three days after the Orillia meeting,
there was a fresh explosion, this time in Montreal.

For a lump of cosmetic designed to portray the NDP as
a truly national party, the Quebec section seemed to have
truly carcinogenic properties. Delighted at securing the
earlier agreement from the Laliberté group, party leaders
overlooked the fact that the Quebec party now felt
entitled, as a sympathetic commentator observed, "to
preach doctrines about the future of Canada, to say
nothing about economic and social policies, which may
raise goose flesh in the rest of Canada." And that was
precisely what the Quebec party proceeded to do. While
the main party produced its own "mini-programme" or
platform, Laliberté and Boudreau drafted theirs. Entitled
Il faut prendre le pouvoir partout it flaunted the phrase
"self-determination" at the head of every section. One
especially troublesome passage assured readers that when
Quebec decided on independence, NDPers in Ottawa
would be their most valuable spokesmen. An appalled
David Lewis needed no reminder of the significance of that
sentiment to his opponents in every part of Canada. On
June 26th, the NDP federal officers pleaded in vain for a
delay in publication. Three days later, when the booklet
was presented to the press, Lewis announced his formal
repudiation. For a month, there was a stand-off but both
sides had bargaining counters. Without Laliberté's help,
there would be no more than a handful of NDP candidates
for the seventy-five Quebec seats: without Lewis's formal
approval, not a single candidate could place the NDP label

on the ballot. While party officials put aside a host of more urgent preoccupations, negotiations resumed. Finally, a patchwork compromise was accepted. Then there were further delays but, in mid-September, a poorly-attended special convention of the Quebec NDP accepted the amendments with an ill grace.

It was a bleak beginning to an election campaign for which the NDP had had more than four years to prepare. A year before, the party had even sneaked ahead of the Conservatives in the Gallup ratings — though only at twenty-four per cent to an abysmal Tory standing of twenty-three per cent. On the eve of the 1972 election, in August, the polls indicated only fifteen per cent support for the NDP. Editors had enjoyed themselves through the summer excoriating the heartless treatment of the Waffle and revelling in the party's plight in Quebec. A party survey, piggybacked on a Gallup poll, indicated in February that support was down in British Columbia and, when Premier Bennett called a surprise summer election, it seemed that the party would find little comfort in the outcome. There was only modest reassurance in a Vancouver *Province* survey suggesting that the NDP stood at a high of thirty-four per cent support among provincial voters. Abandoning a license surely forgiveable in opposition leaders, Dave Barrett forbade party supporters to announce him as the next premier of British Columbia. Why defy credulity?

In fact, though few knew it, Barrett was busy making himself the next premier of British Columbia and beating the unbeatable W. A. C. Bennett into the bargain. Berger, with moderation, patience and systematic organization, had failed. Barrett, with a scratch organization, more limited funds and a bravura personality, succeeded. Berger had tried to ignore Bennett's charges of revolutionary socialism; Barrett laughed them out of the hall. "If he calls me a Waffle," he joked, "I'll call him a pancake. If he calls me a double Waffle, I'll call him a stack of pancakes. And if he keeps calling me a Waffler, knowing his attitude to Quebec, I'll call him a crêpe suzette." When the premier warned that the socialist hordes were at the gates, bumper stickers appeared, boasting of the fact. The tactics worked, partly because Dave Barrett was in the flamboyant tradition British Columbians have always admired in politicians since Richard McBride, Duff Pattullo and Bennett himself; partly because the province was eager for a change. The gas in the durable Social Credit balloon had been prosperity, full employment and ample public works. Now, unemployment was rising, the province's resource industries seemed to be in the doldrums and Bennett, to aggravate matters, had antagonised most of the pressure groups in the province, from organized labour to the school teachers. Even business was disenchanted and, in the young Conservative leader, Derril Warren, it thought it had an alternative.

On the night of August 30th, the longest provincial struggle for democratic socialism in Canada entered a new phase. A shocked, slightly exhilarated province discovered that it had given the ebullient Barrett thirty-eight seats and almost forty per cent of the popular vote. Only ten seats were left for Social Credit, five for the Liberals and a meagre two for the Conservatives.

Within a few weeks, the 41-year old social worker had formed his government, spreading portfolios across the factions of the party, summoned the new legislature and demonstrated that a new era had come to British Columbia. A tenants' bill of rights, plans for urban rapid transit, a ward system for Vancouver and a guaranteed $200 income for old age pensioners were all hurried into law. The province's wealthy mining and forest industries learned that the era of sweetheart royalty deals was over and the insurance industry discovered that Barrett had plans to go even farther into public insurance than Saskatchewan and Manitoba.

The British Columbia victory, on the eve of the twenty-ninth federal election, could not have come at a better moment for a divided and depressed party. It was not the only fillip for the party faithful. In a month-long pre-election tour, David Lewis had developed the issue which suddenly shot him and his party into the running.

Preparations for the 1972 campaign had so far been distinctly lacklustre. The February survey indicated little perceptible improvement in the party's prospects over the 1968 result, no widespread enthusiasm for the NDP's new leader and even greater public disapproval of trade unions than of the Waffle, an organization of which surprisingly few had heard. The party's advertising agency, approached for fresh ideas, could offer only a variant of the 1968 slogan: this time, the party would proclaim "Canada needs More New Democrats." After the Waffle imbroglio and the Quebec conflict, Canadians might reasonably wonder why.

All at once, David Lewis gave them a reason. The previous spring, in an overdue attempt to restore the prosperity Canadians had traditionally associated with Liberal governments, the federal finance minister, John Turner, had announced surprisingly generous tax concessions to corporations. With the promised largesse, free enterprise would presumably create jobs and reduce an embarrassing seven per cent unemployment rate to a more acceptable level. The government's benevolence evoked NDP criticism at the time but it also sent the party's federal research director, Boris Celovsky, digging into other examples of Liberal benevolence to private companies. The result, backed with names, figures and a brilliant slogan, gave Lewis his issue. Launched at a crowded rally in New Glasgow, Nova Scotia, the image of

"Corporate Welfare Bums" penetrated the headlines, sent journalists scurrying along the NDP's pre-campaign trail and delighted party supporters. Whatever its effect in converting masses of voters — it was minimal — the corporate tax rip-off was the kind of issue which only a party like the NDP could raise. Thousands of party members who had forgotten why they belonged suddenly remembered. Editors and journalists, delighted to find snap and crackle in the early stages of a dull campaign, gave the NDP unprecedented publicity. Party researchers, in turn, became so entranced with the so-called corporate rip-off that they stopped in mid-campaign to put together a book on the issue.

By then, the issue had begun to pall. Robert Stanfield and his local campaigners shortened the slogan and used it as a sadly effective weapon against the poor and the jobless, insisting that they lived on government largesse. Lewis and his entourage turned slowly back to other, more familiar NDP issues and slogans. Loaded aboard an aged Handley-Page Herald for the last few weeks, the leader's tour at last could claim its own aircraft and an esprit de corps which compensated for an absence of fresh ideas but some of the momentum obviously went out of the campaign.

Perhaps it hardly mattered. As in previous federal contests, the essential NDP campaigns were local constituency battles in which the morale and organization of the party's volunteers could alone help to determine the outcome. For that, the combination of Lewis's fiery attacks on favourite NDP enemies and the thrill of the British Columbia victory were sufficient. In the 1972 election, the party campaigned, almost for the first time, without illusions. Ritual visits to Quebec were brief, sadly disorganized and soon forgotten. Lewis went where the party had votes and the potential for more — to the West, to northern Ontario and the industrialized south, and, fleetingly, to the Atlantic provinces. The NDP campaigned, as it always had, for its only realistic federal goal — an effective balance of power in Parliament. Regularly, as in earlier elections, pre-election punditry predicted that outcome. On October 31st, the experts seemed to be flabbergasted that that was precisely what happened.

In Ottawa, where Mr. Trudeau waited complacently for his majority, there was dismay. In Halifax, where the returns had begun to promise Mr. Stanfield the majority he had privately barely expected, there was a rough, angry disappointment as the prize was pulled away. In Toronto, in the shabby ballroom where defeated NDP candidates and their workers had come to share the smell of victory with the lucky few, there was a mixture of exultation and realism. 1,7000,000 Canadians, 18.1 per cent of the voters, had given Parliament more New Democrats — thirty-one of them, even one from the huge, empty North-West Territories. Could they justify the trust?

VIII. Epilogue

Contemporary history is always an unfinished story, scuffing at the heels of the present. Confident projections of the future turn out to be straight-line graphs to nowhere. There can be no tidy conclusions. By the beginning of 1974, the verdict on Canada's Twenty-Ninth Parliament was not yet in. Saskatchewan voters had yet to pass judgement on the Blakeney government and British Columbia was still getting used to the tempestuous presence of Dave Barrett and his "socialist hordes."

Only in Manitoba had the NDP been tested. In 1969 Ed Schreyer had promised, if allowed, that he would complete a full four year term. He kept his promise. On June 28th, 1973, Manitobans could decide the fate of their first really radical government in more than half a century. Against the legislative turmoil and occasional bungle, voters could set the experience of a government which had kept its promises without running the province into bankruptcy. In fact, for people earning less than $20,000 a year — and that was most Manitobans — taxes were lower than in 1969.

Would-be saviours of the free enterprise system wheeled and wheedled behind the scenes, trying to persuade Liberal and Conservative voters to gang up on the NDP. Winnipeg

◁ Dave Barrett. A shocked, slightly exhilarated province discovered that the longest provincial struggle for democratic socialism was over. The flamboyant tradition of Richard McBride and Duff Pattullo had found a new standard-bearer. (United Steelworkers)

newspapers pleaded with Manitobans to undo the damage
they had done four years before. In an odd counterpoint,
voters got the same message from Joe Borowski, now
running as a law and order independent and from the
doctrinaire Cy Gonick, who had flounced out of politics
altogether.

Their advice had little discernible impact. Election day
revealed a four per cent increase in popular support for
Schreyer and his government, a one per cent gain for the
Conservatives and a mere nineteen per cent support for
I. H. Asper's Liberals. Schreyer got thirty-one seats, his
opponents twenty-six, though several contests were close
enough to be settled by the courts. It was sufficient to
show that an NDP government was no longer an aberration
in what had once seemed one of Canada's most
conservative provinces.

Across western Canada, three governments in widely
differing provinces gave a better idea of what the NDP was
about than the mountain of speeches and resolutions
accumulated since 1961. Schreyer, Blakeney and Barrett
were as diverse in background, style and outlook as their
respective provinces but they shared a common orientation
away from dogma and toward practical programmes. If
they had a vision of socialism, they would move toward it
with the support of a minimum of forty per cent of the
electorate. That meant a steady diet of social democratic
policies, each designed to stand on its own merits.

For example, with governments involved in automobile
insurance in all three provinces and venturing into fire
insurance in two of them, the NDP obviously has access to
rich investment funds for its development policies.
However, the pay-off to voters has to come in the form of
reduced premiums and better service. All three NDP
governments have concentrated on improved welfare payments and services. Manitoba's Pharmacare drug coverage

for the elderly has been imitated by British Columbia and the other provinces are already following its lead in providing free dental care for children. British Columbia's Mincome programme guarantees a minimum of $209 a month for the elderly, an example for wealthier provinces like Ontario to imitate. The coast province's minimum wage, currently $2.50 an hour, is the highest in the world.

Income redistribution and social insurance programmes are not exclusively socialist ideas, although social democrats have normally had to lead the fight for them in Canada. A more familiar touchstone has been enthusiasm for public ownership. In this domain, Canadian socialists have not had a monopoly. Conservatives take credit for Ontario Hydro and the CNR, Liberals created Air Canada and most of the crown corporations; even Social Credit in British Columbia nationalized the ferries and B.C. Hydro without batting an eye. More common has been the arrangement which Ed Schreyer has dismissed as "mongrel enterprise," in which taxpayers provide most of the capital and shareholders get all of the profits. That principle built the C.P.R. in the 1880s, maintained Denison Mines in the 1960s and kept much of Canadian business happy in the intervening years. It reflects a free enterprise dogma that a government has no right to make a profit.

Canada's three NDP governments have given little apparent allegiance to either doctrinaire socialist or free enterprise principles. Schreyer's most disastrous inheritance, Churchill Forest Industries, was a model mongrel enterprise, with Manitobans providing millions of dollars in a partnership with shadowy capitalists hidden behind a numbered Swiss bank account. In Saskatchewan, the Blakeney government took over just in time to stop what might have become a comparable adventure. Like other Canadian governments, the NDP administrations still put public money into private companies; unlike the others, the NDP insists on the same kind of equity and voice in management that any other prudent investor would demand. One damaging result is that voters now learn what they gain or lose by their investments, and in Manitoba's case, propping up ailing industries has sometimes been expensive. In Ontario and the Atlantic provinces, the voters' ignorance of the fate of grants and "forgiveable" loans is the politicians' bliss.

In all three NDP provinces, public ownership has been less an ideological imperative, more a convenient policy tool. British Columbia, the wealthiest, has been able to afford the greatest flair. When a boardroom decision condemned the pulp and paper town of Ocean Falls to sudden death, the Barrett government planked down a million dollars to buy the entrie complex – just as world pulp and paper prices started a phenomenal leap. Instead of nationalizing British Columbia's privately-owned telephone company, as the NDP had promised, Barrett waited while share prices plummeted. As they hit bottom, he moved in to buy large blocks, moving toward control at bargain basement prices. Party purists, incidentally, were outraged at a socialist playing the stock market.

In the rural areas of Manitoba and Saskatchewan, the smaller family farm has been fighting a losing battle against the encroachment of vertically-integrated corporate farming. Liberal and Conservative governments had publicly moaned about their inability to meddle in the free market and privately confessed that the small operator was a hopeless anachronism. The Schreyer and Blakeney governments have been willing to defy market determinism. Manitoba's "Stay" programme used public funds to buy up farms, retiring their aged owners and making land available to younger farmers who wanted to get started or to expand their operations. Producer-controlled marketing boards, cheaper crop insurance, a Farm Machinery Act to compel implement dealers to stock spare parts, and even funds to revive struggling prairie towns, have all been aspects of the fight to save the family farm. They also contributed to Schreyer's re-election in 1973. In neighbouring Saskatchewan, the Farmstart programme and a controversial land banking system aimed at a similar goal. A subsidiary target was saving Saskatchewan farm land from American-based farming corporations.

Helping small producers to preserve their life-style and, probably, their rural conservatism may seem an odd priority for a left-wing party, but such policies reflect a durable conservationist streak in Canadian social democracy. NDP victories in all three western provinces owed a lot to the claim that irreplaceable natural resources were being disposed of at fire sale prices to greedy foreign entrepreneurs. In office, problems often seem tougher than in opposition. Long-term prosperity for western Canada, perhaps even economic survival, will be the reward for sensible resource development policies, but democratic governments have to deliver in the short-term too. If multinational corporations are not the omnipotent giants of current myth, they do have alternative sources of supply. Miners, loggers and process workers know that their jobs are on the line if their NDP government miscalculates. They, not the chorus of academics and journalists shouting "sell-out" from the sidelines, will be doing the belt-tightening.

The worldwide energy and materials shortage which developed during 1973 gave the western provinces a powerful, if temporary, bargaining position. All three NDP governments have used their opportunity to extract higher royalties and license fees and to expand public involvement in resource industries. Saskoil, financed by greatly increased revenues from existing wells, will be doing most of Saskatchewan's petroleum exploration in coming years while Manitoba's Mineral Resources Ltd. will be leading that province's hunt for new ore bodies. In British Columbia, the Barrett government boosted resource taxes, squeezed out less efficient enterprises and took them over. By the end of 1973, two out of three acquisitions were making money.

To a greater degree than the NDP comfortably admits, the rest of Canada has been paying the price for higher cost western resources, from wheat to wood pulp. For the party, whose repertoire of federal-provincial issues once seemed limited to the grievances of Quebec, this forced a new awareness of economic as well as cultural strains in Confederation. For the NDP, resolving regional differences with a web of socialist rhetoric became a lot more difficult when the the NDP actually formed governments and when a tough, articulate politician like Allan Blakeney spoke for an entire province and not simply for a provincial caucus. Like other Canadian parties, the NDP has now had to face the unfamiliar experience of hard inter-regional bargaining, particularly in reconciling its national and provincial oil policies.

Since October 30th, 1972, David Lewis and his thirty NDP colleagues in Ottawa have also represented rather more than a third party. Holding the balance in a parliament of minorities (a task shared with the Créditistes from 1962 to 1968) brought more responsibility than power. Press gallery experts and frustrated Conservatives regularly denounced the NDP for keeping the Trudeau government in office and scolded the party for allowing its ideas to be stolen by the Liberals. The NDP could only reply that there is no copyright on common sense. Even more infuriating was the regular reminder that most government decisions, from the appointment of a chairman for the Food Prices Review Board to the recognition of a military junta in Chile, were made in the secrecy of the cabinet, not in Parliament.

However, the NDP took its chances, generally kept its head, and forced enough highly-publicised confrontations with the government to take credit for some of its abrupt changes of direction. By the end of 1973, Lewis and his colleagues could boast of higher old age pensions and family allowances, subsidies to control the price of bread and milk, significant reform of the law governing election contributions and the prospect of a national energy policy which bore at least a family resemblance to the party's own ideas. If the party had lost its battle against corporate tax concessions, the main issue in its 1972 campaign, it was largely because the Tories, for all their professed desire to defeat the government, had found discretion the better part of valour.

Still, it had been a difficult, dangerous year. In two successive general elections, the NDP had campaigned for precisely the kind of influential position it enjoyed in the Twenty-Ninth Parliament. For a party limited, effectively, to four provinces and the Northwest Territories, what more was possible? Yet, at times, its members seemed to be as dubious as the editorial writers about the legitimacy of a minority government. Oddly enough, the nervous M.Ps. could take comfort from the opinion polls: with NDP standings at or slightly above the 1972 result, it seemed that the party's voters understood what was happening. So did the party rank and file. Instead of the expected apocalyptic rage, the NDP's federal convention in Vancouver in the summer of 1973 was so quiet, reasonable and productive that journalists who had headed west for the usual fun almost wondered how to justify their expense claims.

Part of the explanation for a new maturity and patience was the presence of three provincial premiers; part was due to the deliberate departure of much of the NDP's organized left wing. In Ontario, leaders of the Movement for an Independent Socialist Canada (MISC) grew tired of their near-eclipse from the news media and began slipping broad hints of a return to electoral politics. So did their cousins in Saskatchewan. John Richards, a university lecturer and M.L.A., abandoned the NDP caucus to become leader, spokesman and sole representative of a new "Waffle" party. In both provinces, reaction from former sympathisers with the Waffle was generally frosty. As for the "crazies," as Mel Watkins had termed the radical dissenters from his own leadership, most returned briefly to the Ontario NDP, disrupted much of the party's 1972 convention, and disappeared again into the "Revolutionary Marxist Group."

In Ontario, a year after the Waffle conflict, little damage was evident. By the summer of 1973, the party had gathered 23,900 members and had persuaded them to give enough money to pay off debts dating back to 1968. A badly shaken Stephen Lewis withdrew from public view, debated his political future and allowed the public to forget his aggressive image. By the time he emerged, most of the party faithful seemed persuaded that he was, in fact, the man they wanted as leader.

Across Canada, the New Democratic Party no longer lived with the nightmare fear of early oblivion: three provincial governments were a guarantee that social democracy mattered in Canada. Vastly more had been accomplished at the provincial level than the drafters of the Regina Manifesto could have dreamed, and even victory in Ontario might seem possible.

However, provincial victories could only be way-stations for the NDP's advance on Ottawa. Without desperately needed national and even international policies of economic stabilization and equalization, even provincial footholds could be jeopardised. Federal success still depends on the NDP's unfulfilled goal — making substantial headway in both Ontario and Quebec. In the former province, progress has at least been perceptible; in the latter, the NDP faces a more intractable problem. West of the Ottawa River and particularly on the prairies, the NDP could build on a shared concept of popular sovereignty which bred suspicion of business and professional elites. To the extend that such a mood ever existed in French Canada, it has been mobilized by the Créditistes. In the absence of a populist or even a labourist political tradition, the NDP in Quebec and, to some extent, in the Atlantic provinces, has been confined to a share of the intellectual elite. Inevitably and perhaps fatally it has absorbed the preoccupations of that elite. In the Seventies, the NDP must choose between futility and the exhausting and dangerous business of finding roots in new soil east of the Ottawa river.

Neither the responsibilities of government nor the search for power have relieved the NDP of another responsibility — service as a transmission belt between new ideas and the Canadian political system. In the Seventies, this may be a task of increasing difficulty. Confidence in the old British and Scandinavian sources is declining and the NDP will be compelled to do more of its own thinking about practical applications of its ideals. One of the most acute problems it will face is how liberty and equality can both be enhanced in a world confronted by scarcity of every kind of resource. "(I)f abundance is not possible," Michael Harrington has warned, "then neither is socialism and there is no reformulation that can evade that fact." It is a chilling warning from the continent's most distinguished democratic socialist thinker but any alternative definition of socialism, based on rationing, controls, bureaucracy and the images of *1984* can only be concocted by enemies. The prospect of scarcity challenges most of the assumptions about growth and the potential of technological achievement which have sustained socialism into our own era. Realizing the ideals without the expected means will demand incredible faith and ingenuity.

* * *

Thirteen years have passed since the rapturous excitement of the Founding Convention, more than sixteen since the original decision to attempt the New Party experiment. As a coalition designed to appeal to trade unionists, to middle-class liberals and to that uneasy alliance of idealists and pragmatic radicals who had already made their home in the CCF, the new party had been a slate on which everyone could write their own impressions. By 1974, with three provincial governments in office and an NDP caucus in Ottawa compelled to make choices as well as speeches, the New Democratic Party had a shape and a definition.

Part of its shape is its structure. To New Democrats, it is almost the most unique feature of their party. The old parties, they insist, are autocratic organizations in which policy is determined by a leader's whim, membership is sold at the door of nominating conventions and money is collected by discreet bagmen. In the NDP, on the contrary, policies are adopted by the members, leaders must renew their mandates at regular conventions, and financial support is provided openly by hundreds of thousands of Canadians.

Within the limits of over-simplification and some wishful thinking, the contrast between the party and its opponents has validity. Democracy in the NDP does not suspend the normal rules of political behaviour. Leaders are fond of having their own way. Majorities shirk their obligation to sit through tiresome meetings and minorities complain that freedom has been trampled when they do not get their way.

Democracy depends, basically, on membership participation. The NDP would like to be regarded as a "mass" party and its criteria for membership are modest. Unlike some earlier Canadian socialist parties which imposed examinations on applicants, would-be New Democrats need only be residents of Canada, over fourteen years of age and not "a member of supporter of any other political party." The exclusion is more often raised against Communists and Trotskyites than against errant Liberals or Tories. Otherwise, members are welcomed, provided with a card and urged to attend the meetings, educational sessions, dances, socials and other activities which ideally mark the membership year. Annual fees, together with sustaining contributions in excess of the basic amount, are forwarded to the provincial office where half the amount is retained. The rest is divided evenly between the federal NDP and a member's own association. A complicated fee structure, division of funds between three levels of the party and other organizational transactions have persuaded at least two provincial sections to keep their membership records in a computer. Currently, there are about 73,000 individual New Democrats, 25,000 in Saskatchewan, 25,000 in Ontario and most of the rest in British Columbia, Manitoba, Nova Scotia and Alberta.

A more controversial feature of NDP structure is affiliated membership. Theoretically open to any kind of organization, from a credit union to a ratepayers' association, the option has been exercised by a handful of left-wing study groups and by a large number of local trade unions, ranging from the thirty-eight firefighters of Cornerbrook, Newfoundland, to the enormous Steelworkers' local in Sudbury. Most come with the blessing of union leaders; a few have defied national or international headquarters by joining. The NDP's own rules require affiliation to be approved by a general membership meeting and for opponents to be allowed to opt out. In practice, unions affiliate for only a proportion of their members, saving dissenters the need to make themselves known. The affiliation fee — ten cents per member per month — is paid directly to the federal NDP which keeps six cents and forwards the balance to the respective provincial organization. There were about 275,000 affiliated members in 1973.

The NDP has perhaps been needlessly sensitive about the propriety of union affiliation. Obviously some members of affiliates support other political parties, though their proportion has fallen during the Sixties. Instances of disaffiliation are rare and resolutions of support for the NDP at national and provincial labour conventions have become *pro forma*. Perhaps, as Gad Horowitz argues in *Canadian Labour in Politics*, it is not "nice" to admit that Canadian politics have been based on group identification or that Liberals and Conservatives appeal specifically to ethnic, religious and economic groups. Some abuses of union political participation, such as the British Labour Party's bloc vote, which places the support of a union membership entirely on one side or the other of a conference decision, are unknown in the NDP.

The NDP has generally abandoned attempts to maintain special federal organizations for women and youth supporters. While some provincial organizations retain such traditional political institutions, general NDP experience seems to be that the abler members of both groups find their opportunities in the main party institutions, leaving women's groups and youth clubs to collapse or as a prey to outside infiltration.

In overall structure, the New Democratic Party of Canada is a federation of largely autonomous provincial parties. The Sixties have seen a steady devolution of activity and influence, particularly to the five provincial sections west of the Ottawa river. Provincial parties are wholly responsible for their own membership and finances, for federal as well as provincial elections and for organization, education, publicity and any other activities for which they have time, energy and resources. Relations with the five eastern provinces are qualified by their dependence on party subsidies, their structural weakness and the occasional outbursts of factionalism which, as in most organizations, vary inversely with size. Like the CCF before it, the federal NDP receives the lion's share of its revenue from Ontario and Saskatchewan, and even victory in Manitoba and British Columbia has not notably increased these provinces' share of the central burden. One consequence is that the central office of the party is chronically under-financed.

Like the federal NDP, most provincial parties maintain an office, a full-time secretary and a permanent staff to process memberships, keep records and serve the party's committees. In the stronger provinces, a cadre of professional organizers helps spur constituency organization, promotes affiliation and develops election and community workers.

The governing structure for the federal NDP and for most of its provincial sections is roughly identical. Officially, the supreme body is an annual or (in Ontario and federally) biennial convention. Representation is based on a proportion of membership in constituencies and affiliated organizations, without the discriminatory clauses on sex and age imposed by the traditional parties. The federal NDP allows a delegate for every fifty individual members of a riding association and a delegate for each thousand members of an affiliated organization. Attendance tends to be limited by the cost of registration fees (conventions have to be self-financing) and by travel expenses. Normally, constituency delegates outnumber union delegates

by about two to one, though some riding representatives are themselves unionists in good standing.

As an over-all policy-making body, an NDP convention can have serious limitations. Gatherings may be as large as a thousand or more delegates. Even after winnowing by an influential resolutions committee, scores of complex and controversial matters come before a single convention and part of the explanation for the NDP's notorious verbosity is its desire to cover as many anticipated viewpoints as possible. Ordinary delegates, largely unaware of the back-room bustle, thumb through mountains of printed and mimeographed resolutions (in both official languages at federal conventions), lose their places, get distracted and often end up voting on cue from more experienced neighbours. The mood is almost always purposeful and a little solemn — NDP conventions are rarely excuses for jollification or pep rallies — but sometimes there is bewilderment and frustration as well. In the smaller provincial sections, conventions are still as intimate and familiar as in CCF days, but the party's larger gatherings have tended to become unwieldy, ineffective and vulnerable to prcedural exhibitionists or to organized disruption, such as occurred at the Ontario 1972 convention. As policy forums, conventions have worked best during formal debates, as on the rival manifestos in Winnipeg in 1969 or on "self-determination" in Ottawa in 1971. The arguments can be clearly presented, delegates have an adequate chance to decide what is at stake: the chief disadvantage is an artificially heightened atmosphere of polarization.

Probably an NDP convention's most important power is its right to choose or reaffirm leaders. Resolutions may vanish in the mass of words which the NDP tends to generate; a leader goes on to become the personal embodiment of even the most decentralized and anti-

◁ The prospects for the New Democratic Party will depend, in large measure, on its ability to attract younger Canadians without losing the support of traditional left-wing voters or the party's working class constituency. (Information Canada)

hierarchical party. No quantity of policy resolutions can
anticipate the daily issues on which party leaders must
take stands and on which their party will most often be
judged. The selection of a leader is a critical choice of
image, tactical judgement and, probably, of political
direction. In *Political Parties*, Robert Michels commented
on the durability of European socialist leaders and he
might well have extended his principle to the CCF – NDP.
So far, no incumbent leader has actually been defeated by
an NDP federal or provincial convention, but the prospect
of a divisive and possibly successful challenge has led to at
least one leadership change in each NDP provincial section
since 1961.

More effective than the convention as a forum for
democratic control of the NDP is the federal or provincial
council. At the former, provincial delegates predominate;
at the latter, constituency associations are represented, and
in both bodies there is a limited trade union representation. Meeting three or four times a year, with most of their
members familiar with party affairs, councils tend to be
more knowledgeable and consistent in debate and more
penetrating in calling leaders to account. Though in theory
subordinate to a convention, an NDP council can do
almost anything but choose a new party leader. Meetings
adopt policy statements, scrutinise budgets and reports,
hear occasional appeals from decisions on party discipline
and provide at least a preliminary judgement on matters of
serious controversy within the party.

Federal and provincial executives in the NDP consist of
a number of officers elected by the convention and
additional members elected by the council (except in
Ontario where all but two youth members are chosen
directly by the convention). Executives meet from six to
eight times a year and, with their committees, form the
central authority structure for the party and its sections.

Despite occasional pressure, the NDP has generally rejected attempts to impose specific quotas of, for example, women or trade unionists in its executives. Instead, balance is sought through the institution of the "slate," a list of candidates for executive office balanced informally, in the time-honoured Canadian way, by region, sex, age and economic status. A variety of slates appear at conventions, sponsored by groups ranging from the current party leadership to those representing the party's "left wing." Normally most members of the "official" slate are successful but one or two others usually manage to "break the slate" and thus join the party establishment.

For most practical purposes, provincial sections of the NDP are divided into constituency associations. Normally, provincial boundaries serve as the geographic basis and federal constituencies are organized *ad hoc* by committees. This is frequently an awkward and unsatisfactory arrangement, reinforcing the increasing provincial orientation of the NDP, but the party has taken pride in operating equally at all levels of politics. As a general rule, it lacks the resources and leadership to operate effective parallel organizations.

Electoral candidates are chosen only by party members living within the constituency and the Canadian tradition of packing nominating meetings by last-minute recruiting drives is discouraged by a two-week cut-off date for new members. To safeguard party principles, candidates must be endorsed by the party's provincial council and, in federal elections, the federal party may also intervene to nullify the nomination of a candidate whose allegiance to NDP principles or policies is considered dubious. Federal party approval has become more significant with the addition of party names to the ballot and the 1974 amendments to the law on election finance. In fact, formal interference has been rare although a few would-be candidates have been quietly warned that they were unlikely to be approved.

Like other Canadians, New Democrats tend to feel that the choice of a candidate is a local prerogative, though constituencies which have difficulty in finding a suitable nominee can usually appeal to their provincial organization. Similarly, with cautious diplomacy, provincial NDP officials may seek to "place" a candidate with impressive credentials but no home base. Federally and provincially, the party may also compel a constituency association to present a candidate although, again, such coercion has been rare. Like other parties, the NDP has made a special effort to field qualified women candidates; unlike its rivals, it has also sought out able trade unionists. In both cases, experience in winning electoral support has been discouraging.

Election campaings illustrate the financial and organizational interdependence of the NDP structure. Though the federal party has direct access to the head-offices of sympathetic unions while riding associations can tap members, supporters and local affiliates, the provincial level of the NDP has few direct sources of funds. Some provincial headquarters have imposed a tithe or quota on constituencies amounting to twenty per cent of their election budgets. After a weak response in the early Sixties, quota payments have become a significant source of revenue, providing up to two-thirds of the election fund in a province like Ontario. Such financing is a contrast to the practices of other political parties which normally collect most funds centrally and distribute them to constituencies. One result of reliable sources and cautious spending is that the NDP, almost alone among political parties, can maintain a favourable credit rating.

Among party fundamentalists, the NDP's preoccupation with elections and parliamentary politics is a regular source of complaint. In their view, the party should devote more of its resources to community organizing, rallying support for the procession of causes which catch the fancy of the Left, from banning the Bomb to liberating abortionists. The problem is that elections and legislatures are the NDP's primary business, commanding all the energy and funds the party can muster, particularly when municipal contests are added to federal and provincial campaigns. By the time the party has managed to respond to one of the current issues, it usually finds that one or more of the totalitarian factions of the Left have devised a front group for the issue. The NDP has not, in practice, seriously attempted to provide its members with a comprehensive political life.

In itself, that suggests a structural problem with which the NDP has yet to come to grips. In his study of the CCF, Walter Young emphasized the continuing conflict of the "movement" and "party" elements. Socialist purists in the CCF regularly wrestled with pragmatists whose main concern was to win public acceptance for at least some socialist ideas. The same dichotomy is useful in any analysis of the internal divisions within the NDP but there is also another important split — between the party's active membership, represented by its structure, and its electorate, represented by its M.Ps, M.L.As, and three provincial governments.

Except, perhaps, for Saskatchewan where the NDP membership is large enough to form a significant bloc of the population, the party structure can hardly claim to reflect the massive party electorate. Manitoba's mere 1,200 active 1973 members represent less than one per cent of the NDP's 194,705 voters in the 1973 election. Even British Columbia's 12,000 New Democrats form a mass party more in theory than in practice. As a result, governments have to weigh the passionate opinions of a few hundred convention delegates against their assessment of the collective will of an entire electorate.

The 1,700,000 Canadians who vote for the NDP or the forty-odd per cent who keep the NDP in office in Manitoba, Saskatchewan and British Columbia are probably not, for the most part, those on whom Liberals and Conservatives can depend. When Ed Schreyer campaigned in 1973 on the slogan "Keep your government *yours*," he was not directing his appeal at the comfortable burghers of River Heights. But neither was he directing it at the editors of *Canadian Dimension* or the more radical academics of the University of Manitoba. His government, he insisted, represented more people than the party. In British Columbia, Dave Barrett made the same point to disgruntled trade unionists.

The NDP's pride in its democratic structure is merited. The party is distinctive among Canadian political organizations in the degree and maturity of its internal responsiveness. However political relationships are based on power, not theory, and a party which has failed to develop a strong and representative membership base will have only a feeble claim to influence the policy of even a sympathetic government. It cannot, for example, honestly claim to reflect widespread public feeling and it will lack the strength to convert public feeling to the party's views. If Manitoba New Democrats complain, as they frequently do, that the Schreyer government fails to match their own standards of radicalism, their remedy lies in developing the same kind of mass membership party as neighbouring Saskatchewan. Governments, in turn, must realize that their fate may depend on the availability of committed volunteers, ready to carry the battle to the doorsteps. Neither electorates nor party structures are dispensable: both must somehow be persuaded that the NDP is "their" party.

For members, if not necessarily for voting supporters, allegiance to the NDP will involve a vision of a better society. Like the CCF, the NDP has neither promised nor delivered revolutionary transformations; critics and supporters who claimed otherwise deceived themselves and others. The party's general rejection of doctrinaire solutions has not been a mask for acceptance of present social and economic conditions. New Democrats see poverty as a state to be eliminated, not merely made endurable. They want people to have a direct voice in determining their own destiny, not simply to serve in the cheering section.

It is a valid criticism of the NDP that, like other political movements in the social democratic tradition, it does not always see a clear route to these goals. Its policies of social insurance, income redistribution, partial public ownership and assertion of civil liberties, are piecemeal, incomplete and sometimes dull. Social democracy's reply to its totalitarian critics is that their policies have been frequently cruel and often catastrophic. Police terror, slave camps, mass "liquidation" have not been Stalinist or Leninist deviations: their horrifying survival in the Soviet Union and other Communist countries demonstrates that they are an inherent feature of the totalitarian route to social change. To social democrats, it might be better to do nothing than to share in such appalling crimes.

Fortunately, as both the CCF and the NDP have demonstrated, it is possible to do a great deal. Socialism has meant to the NDP in large measure what it meant to J. S. Woodsworth: a belief that the brotherhood of man could be established in the social, economic and political realm. It was a socialism born out of both the Protestant and Catholic social gospel, mixed with a pioneer belief that, in a new land, anything is possible. It could define itself, in John Wilson's phrase, as "a society of friends."

A political faith that is more decided about its goals

than about the routes to them depends on an almost limitless faith in human reason. When one ventures into the uncharted territory of the future without the convenience of a blueprint, bible or chart, one assumes that sufficient intelligence will be available to resolve the problems encountered. True believers may have a selected list of prophets; social democrats must benefit from them all.

It could be a great adventure.

Further Reading

Whatever its other deprivations and deficiencies, the Canadian Left cannot complain of scholarly neglect. Its bibliography is long and the cast of participants impressive — among them such ill-matched intellectuals as O. D. Skelton and Stephen Leacock, united only in their determination to refute the spreading hersy of socialism. More numerous are those, like Frank Underhill or Eugene Forsey, who have served a passionate but temporary allegiance to the socialist cause by brilliant journalism.

Those who seek a fuller knowledge of the roots of the Canadian Left may find it in Doris French's unpretentious *Faith, Sweat and Politics*, Toronto, 1962, based on the life of Daniel O'Donoghue, or in Paul Fox's valuable essay, "Early Socialism in Canada," in J. H. Aitchison's *The Political Process in Canada*, Toronto, 1963. Frank Watt looked at labour radicals in "The National Policy, the Working Man and the Proletarian Idea in Victorian Canada," *Canadian Historical Review* 40, 1959. The most thorough account of the background of the Canadian Left is Martin Robin's *Radical Politics and Canadian Labour*, Kingston, 1968.

For all its limitations of datedness and dryness, the only thorough and reputable study of the development of the

Canadian labour movement remains Henry Logan's *Trade Unions in Canada*, Toronto, 1948. Another veteran work is Donald Masters' *The Winnipeg General Strike*, Toronto, 1949, which, despite much revisionist writing, remains the best volume on the topic. Those who seek a briefer account of Canadian labour now may find it in Stuart Jamieson's *Industrial Relations in Canada*, Toronto, 1973, rev. ed., or in the essays in R. U. Miller and Fraser Isbester, *Canadian Labour in Transition*, Scarborough, 1971. Irving Abella's *Nationalism, Communism and Canadian Labour*, Toronto, 1973, is an able, if partisan, account of the struggle between the Communists and the CCF for the control of the CIO unions in Canada.

Other contributing streams in the Canadian left-wing tradition may be studied in W. L. Morton, *The Progressive Party of Canada*, Toronto, 1950, in W. C. Good's *Farmer Citizen: My Fifty Years in the Canadian Farmers' Movement*, Toronto, 1958, and in William Rolph's *Henry Wise Wood of Alberta*, Toronto, 1950. A stream that diverged is studied, in its earlier years, by William Rodney in *Soldiers of the International: A History of the Communist Party of Canada, 1919-1929*, Toronto, 1968.

Much has been written about the CCF in most of its aspects. Kenneth McNaught, *A Prophet in Politics*, Toronto, 1959, has provided a full-length biography of its founder and first leader, J. S. Woodsworth, while Walter Young, a leading figure in the New Party movement, contributed the most important over-all study, *The National CCF: Anatomy of a Party*, Toronto, 1969. The Ontario CCF has been studied by Gerald Caplan in *The Dilemma of Canadian Socialism: The CCF in Ontario, 1932-1945*, Toronto, 1973, while Leo Zakuta, who experienced the party in its later years, has written *A Protest Movement Becalmed*, Toronto, 1964. The tribulations of a CCF leader in Quebec were described by Thérèse

Casgrain in *A Woman in a Man's World*, Toronto, 1971. Apart from Dorothy Steeves' *The Compassionate Rebel: Ernest Winch and His Times*, Vancouver, 1960, there is disappointingly little about the CCF in British Columbia, though Martin Robin's *The Pillars of Profit*, Toronto, 1973, sets the party in its political context. The contribution of the CCF's intellectuals has been set down by Michiel Horn in "The League for Social Reconstruction and the Development of a Canadian Socialism, 1932-1936," *Journal of Canadian Studies* 7, 1972, while some of the work of its most prolific member, Frank Underhill, may be read in *In Search of Canadian Liberalism*, Toronto, 1960.

The CCF's major achievements were in Saskatchewan. The most thorough study of the prairie phenomenon is S. M. Lipset's *Agrarian Socialism: The Co-operative Commonwealth Federation in Saskatchewan*, Los Angeles, 1967, rev. ed. A more popular account, by the late Chris Higinbotham, is *Off The Record: The CCF in Saskatchewan*, Toronto, 1968. Some aspects of CCF government as seen by insiders can be found in Laurier LaPierre et al, eds., *Essays on the Left*, Toronto, 1971, while the party's attempt at accountability is discussed by Evelyn Eager, "The Paradox of Power in the Saskatchewan CCF, 1944-1961," in J. H. Aitchison, *op. cit.* The dispute over medical care insurance has been described by Robin Badgley and Samuel Wolfe, *Doctors' Strike: Medical Care and Conflict in Saskatchewan*, Toronto, 1967, and by E. A. Tollefsen, *Bitter Medicine: The Saskatchewan Medicare Dispute*, Saskatoon, 1963.

It is when one approaches the New Democratic Party period that a shortage of informative background reading becomes very apparent. The most useful book is Gad Horowitz's study of the twenty-year process by which the trade union movement was brought to share in the new party, *Canadian Labour in Politics*, Toronto, 1968. Horowitz has also provided a provocative essay on why socialism has seemed possible in Canada but not in the United States. *The New Party*, Toronto, 1961, was Stanley Knowles's attempt to introduce the concept to Canadians. It is a valuable reminder of the arguments and a slightly more poignant souvenir of the hopes of one of the most prominent architects of the new party movement. Otherwise, the NDP finds its minor place in other treatments of Canadian politics in the 1960s, from John Meisel to Peter Newman, from newspaper editorials to the pages of a revived *Canadian Annual Review* which, fortunately, began to appear in 1960. Among the few scholarly articles of relevance are R. U. Miller, "Organized Labour and Politics in Canada" in Miller and Isbester, *op. cit.*; Desmond Morton, "The Effectiveness of Political Campaigning: The NDP in the 1967 Ontario Election," *Journal of Canadian Studies* 4, 1969; and John Wilson, "The Politics of Social Class in Canada: The Case of Waterloo South," *Canadian Journal of Political Science* 1, 1968.

The ideas which have influenced the NDP have been rather more amply recorded. Michael Oliver (ed.), *Social Purpose for Canada*, Toronto, 1961, provided the fledgling party with a rich variety of advice. It was followed, in due course, by a number of books sponsored by the University League for Social Reform, the most important of which were probably Abraham Rotstein (ed.) *The Prospect of Change*, Toronto, 1965, and T. O. Lloyd and J. T. McLeod, (eds), *Agenda 1970: Prospects for a Creative Politics*, Toronto, 1968. Rotstein's attempt to popularize the views of Gunnar Adler-Karlsson, *Reclaiming the Canadian Economy: A Swedish Approach Through Functional Socialism*, Toronto, 1970, had an impact as did Kari Levitt's *Silent Surrender: The Recolonization of Canada*, Toronto, 1971. Charles Taylor's *The Pattern of Politics*,

Toronto, 1970, argued for a more polarized Canadian politics in the aftermath of Trudeaumania. The Waffle position can best be found in Dave Godfrey and Mel Watkins, *From Gordon to Watkins to You*, Toronto, 1970, and, in its post-NDP phase, in Robert Laxer (ed.), *Canada Ltd.*, Toronto, 1973. A rather different attempt to re-define the ideology of the Canadian Left was made by John Wilson, "Towards a Society of Friends: Some Reflections on the Meaning of Democratic Socialism," *Canadian Journal of Political Science* 3, 1970.

Since these works, themselves, have been selected from a select list of over two hundred titles, a great many important books and articles have not been mentioned.

Index

Hawthornethwaite, J. H., 10.
health insurance, 15, 24, 34, 46-7, 49, 51, 55, 60, 90, 100, 103, 113.
Hees, George, 54.
Herridge, H. W., 19, 32.
Hesse, Jurgen, x.
Hinman, E. W., 69.
Hitler, Adolph, 14.
Hooke, A. J., 69.
Horowitz, Gad, ix, 25, 156.
hospital insurance, 15.
House of Commons, 11, 32, 85.
housing, 71.
Howard, Frank, 124, 127-8.

"I Believe in Canada," 63.
"Il faut prendre le pouvoir partout," 138.
individualism, 8.
Industrial Workers of the World, 10.
Ingle, Lorne, x.
injunctions, 72.
International Nickel Co., 72.
International Union of Mine, Mill and Smelter Workers, 31, 37.
international unions, 131.
Irvine, William, 11.

Jaffary, Karl, 96.
Japanese-Canadian deportations, 120.
Jewittt, Pauline, 50.
Jodoin, Claude, 28, 31, 80.
Johnson, Samuel, vi.

Kidd, Bruce, 130.
Kierans, Eric, 83.
King, W. L. M., 9, 12, 14.
Kitchener, 88, 96.
Kitimat, 31.
Knights of Labor, 5.
Knowles, Stanley, 18, 19, 28, 86.

Labour Party (British), 10, 17, 28, 90, 132, 156.
labour radicals, 6, 7, 9.
Lachine constituency, 81.
Laliberté, Raymond, 121, 122-3, 126-9, 138-9.
LaPierre, Laurier, 77, 79, 81, 84, 86, 94.

Latin America, 119.
Laurier, Sir Wilfrid, 46.
Lawrence, Allan, 114.
Laxer, James, 92, 96, 97, 124, 127-8, 129-30, 135.
League for Social Reconstruction, 12.
left wing, 19, 20, 24, 44, 89, 90, 92, 94-5, 107, 151, 155. See also Waffle.
Lenin, V. I., 4, 10.
Leninism, 165.
Lépine, A. T., 7.
Levitt, Kari, 91.
Lewis, David, 13, 19, 24, 28, 43, 64, 75, 86, 91, 92, 94, 95, 106; as leadership candidate, 123-8; as leader, 128-9, 137-8, 141-2, 150-1.
Lewis, Michael, 106.
Lewis, Stephen, 53, 75, 83, 86, 88, 108, 109, 110, 114-7, 152; and the Waffle, 130-5.
Liberal party, vi, 5, 6, 7, 9, 11, 14, 21, 29, 33, 47-8, 50, 56, 75, 97, 101, 111, 120, 127, 146-7, 156; and elections, 34, 38, 40-2, 44, 64-5, 66, 80, 82, 84, 141; in British Columbia, 49, 107, 140; in Manitoba, 68, 99-100, 145-6; Ontario, 57, 72, 115-7; in Saskatchewan, 51-2, 69-70, 111, 113, 114.
Lilooet, 69.
Lloyd, Trevor, 71.
Lloyd, Woodrow S., 33, 51-2, 70, 87, 107.
London (England), 21.
London (Ontario), 135.
Loubier, Gabriel, 83.
Lougheed, Peter, 117.

Macaulay, Robert, 53.
McBride, Sir Richard, 140.
MacDermott, Dennis, 97, 109.
Macdonald, David, 30.
MacDonald, Donald C., 48, 50, 71-3, 87, 88, 108, 109, 116, 130.
Macdonald, Sir John A., 5.
MacEwan, Paul, 111.

McGill University, 44, 45, 77, 89, 91.
Mackenzie, Robert, ix.
Maclean's Magazine, 81.
McNaught, K. W., xv, 78.
Macphail, Agnes, 11.
Mahoney, William, 18.
Manifesto for an Independent Socialist Canada — see Waffle Manifesto.
Manitoba, 36, 46, 69, 73, 87, 88, 103-5, 146-50, 164; elections, (1962), 47, (1966) 68, 99, (1969) 99-103, 114, (1973) 145-6.
Maple Leaf Gardens (Toronto) 43, 65.
Marchand, Jean, 64.
Market Opinion Research Ltd., 114.
Marxism, 9, 106.
Medicare crisis in Saskatchewan, 46-7, 67, see also health insurance.
Memorial University, 111.
Mercier, Honoré, 5.
Methodists, 10.
Michels, Robert, 87, 160.
Middlesex South by-election (1969), 108.
Miike, Martha, x.
Millard, Charles, 18.
Mincome programme, 147.
Mineral Resources Ltd., 140.
mining and resource industries, 140-1.
Minnedosa, 99.
Mitchell, Donald, 108, 130.
"mongrel enterprizes," 147.
Montreal, 36, 37, 43, 45, 60, 65, 75, 78, 84, 90, 121, 124, 126, 129.
Montreal Canadiens, v.
Montreal *Star*, 27.
Morin, Roland, 121.
Moscow, 11.
Mosher, A. R., 13.
Mount Royal constituency, 64.
Movement for an Independent Socialist Canada, 135, 151-2.
Mowat, Oliver, 5.
Munsinger, Gerda, 67.
Murray, "Ma," 69.

NDP Now Group, 123, 126-7, 135.
Nanaimo, 45, 76, 105.
Nanaimo-Cowichan-The Islands constituency by-election (1969), 87, 88.
National Committee for the New Party, 20, 21, 23, 28.
"National Policy," the, 5.
nationalism, Canadian, 96-7; Quebec, 76, 90, 119.
native peoples, 55, 129.
natural resources, 65.
New Brunswick, 36, 120, 123, 138.
New Deal (United States), 7.
"New Deal for People," 113.
New Democratic Party, v, vi, vii, ix, 5, 9, 27, 28, 29, 30, 49, 50, 51, 79, 80, 98, 103, 117, 119, 120, 124, 150-1, 152, 153, 154; and community action, 96, 162-3; constitution and structure, 20, 25, 27, 45, 59-60, 89, 154-64; conventions, 157-9, (Founding), 22-8, 37, 44, 57, 124, 154, (second) 44-5, (third) 60-1, (fourth) 75-8, (fifth) 88, 94-5, 107, 127, 159, (sixth) 124-8, 159, (seventh) 151; and elections, 33, 53, 55, 113, (1962) 35-8, (1963) 40-4, (1965) 56, 61-7, (1968) 81-5, (1972) 141-3; federal office 51, 61, 63-4, 67, 79, 85, 157; finance and organization, 35, 41, 61-2, 67, 79, 82, 85, 88, 97-8, 115-6, 137, 155-6; and labour, 22, 23, 29-31, 32, 35, 37, 50, 97, 107, 108-9, 131-2; and leadership, 85, 105-6, 124-5, 128, 159-60; and policies, 23-5, 34, 43-5, 57-9, 63-5, 76-8, 82, 85, 88-91, 94-5, 100, 126-9, 146-54, 159; principles, 3-4, 44-5, 88, 91, 146-54, 165-6; and provinces, 46-9, 67-73, 87, 146-50.
New Democratic Party of Alberta, 75, 117.
New Democratic Party of British Columbia, 55-6, 105-6, 107, 140, 157, 163; and elections, 49-50, 68-9, 106-7, 139-40.

BOOKS IN RELATED AREAS FROM HAKKERT

SOCIAL STUDIES

CITY LIB: PARTIES AND REFORM, by Stephen Clarkson

PROGRAMS IN SEARCH OF A POLICY: LOW INCOME HOUSING IN CANADA, by Michael Dennis and Susan Fish

ENTERPRISE AND NATIONAL DEVELOPMENT: ESSAYS IN CANADIAN BUSINESS AND ECONOMIC HISTORY, edited by Glenn Porter and Robert D. Cuff

MAYOR HOWLAND: THE CITIZENS' CANDIDATE, by Desmond Morton

N.D.P.: THE DREAM OF POWER, by Desmond Morton

Case Studies in Community Action

MARLBOROUGH MARATHON, by J. L. Granatstein

FIGHTING BACK: URBAN RENEWAL IN TREFANN COURT, by Graham Fraser

THE MOVABLE AIRPORT: THE POLITICS OF GOVERNMENT PLANNING, by Sandra Budden and Joseph Ernst

FACULTY OF LAW REVIEW, UNIVERSITY OF TORONTO, VOLUMES 29, 30, 31, 32

HISTORY AND LITERATURE

Historical Papers: Canadian War Museum,
National Museum of Man, National Museums of Canada

THE LAST WAR DRUM: THE NORTH WEST CAMPAIGN OF 1885, by Desmond Morton

VALIANT MEN: CANADA'S VICTORIA CROSS AND GEORGE CROSS WINNERS, edited by John Swettenham

CANADA INVADED: 1775-1776, by George F. G. Stanley

THE CANADIAN GENERAL: SIR WILLIAM OTTER, by Desmond Morton

Publications of the McMaster University Association
For 18th Century Studies

THE VARIED PATTERN: STUDIES IN THE 18TH CENTURY, edited by Peter Hughes, David Williams